AP®
World History
Rapid Review

Special thanks to the following for their contributions to this text: Laura Aitcheson, Sharon Barazani, Steve Bartley, Leslie Buchanan, Matthew Callan, Lana Chiad, Lauren Claus, Jonathan Darrall, M. Dominic Eggert, Tim Eich, Mark Feery, Isabella Furth, Chris Gage, Joanna Graham, Adam Grey, Rebekah Hawthorne, Katy Haynicz-Smith, Peter Haynicz-Smith, Andre Jessee, Rebecca Knauer, Liz Laub, John Magoun, Melissa McLaughlin, Terry McMullen, Emily Moore, Jenn Moore, Kristin Murner, Amira Sa'di, Ethan Underhill, Oscar Velazquez, Lee Weiss, Dan Wittich, and Nina Zhang.

AP® is a registered trademark of the College Board, which was not involved in the production of, and does not endorse, this product.

This publication is designed to provide accurate information in regard to the subject matter covered as of its publication date, with the understanding that knowledge and best practice constantly evolve. The publisher is not engaged in rendering medical, legal, accounting, or other professional service. If medical or legal advice or other expert assistance is required, the services of a competent professional should be sought. To the fullest extent of the law, neither the Publisher nor the Editors assume any liability for any injury and/or damage to persons or property arising out of or related to any use of the material contained in this book.

Published by Kaplan Publishing, a division of Kaplan, Inc.
750 Third Avenue
New York, NY 10017

"Vimala: The Former Courtesan" (Thig 5.2), translated from the *Pāli* by Ṭhānissaro Bhikkhu. *Access to Insight (Legacy Edition)*, http://www.accesstoinsight.org/tipitaka/kn/thig/thig.05.02.than.html. Used with permission.

10 9 8 7 6 5 4 3 2 1

ISBN-13: 978-1-5062-4271-2

Kaplan Publishing print books are available at special quantity discounts to use for sales promotions, employee premiums, or educational purposes. For more information or to purchase books, please call the Simon & Schuster special sales department at 866-506-1949.

TABLE OF CONTENTS

Additional resources available at www.kaptest.com/apbookresources

PART 1

Getting Started

CHAPTER 1

What You Need to Know About the AP World History Exam

INTRODUCTION

Congratulations on your decision to take the Advanced Placement exam in world history! The exam is a big one: its content measures your knowledge of world history from 8000 B.C.E. to the present. In preparing for the AP exam, you certainly will have built a solid foundation of historical knowledge. While this historical knowledge is critical to your learning, keep in mind that rote memorization of facts, dates, and events alone does not ensure success! The AP exam asks you to apply what you've learned at a higher level in order to demonstrate college-level abilities.

That's where this book comes in. This guide offers much more than a review of world history. We'll show you how to marshal your knowledge of world history and put it to brilliant use on the AP exam. We'll explain the ins and outs of the exam structure and question formats, so you won't experience any surprises. We'll even give you reading and writing strategies that successful students use to score higher on the AP exam.

Are you ready for your adventure through the study and mastery of everything AP World History? Good luck!

OVERVIEW OF THE EXAM STRUCTURE

Advanced Placement exams have been around for decades. While the format and content have changed over the years, the basic goal of the AP program remains the same: to give high school students a chance to earn college credit or advanced placement. To do this, a student needs to do two things:

- Find a college that accepts AP scores.
- Score well enough on the exam.

The first part is easy because most colleges accept AP scores in some form or another. The second part requires a little more effort. If you have worked diligently all year in your course work, you've laid the groundwork. The next step is familiarizing yourself with the exam.

What's On the Exam

The main goal of the College Board (the makers of the AP World History exam) is to help students think like a historian. To that end, some skills and methods you'll be expected to demonstrate are:

- analyzing primary and secondary sources
- making historical comparisons
- using reasoning about the context, causation, and continuity over time of major historical developments
- developing historical arguments

The AP World History exam is broken down into six historical periods:

Period	Period Title	Date Range	Weight
1	Technological and Environmental Transformations	to 600 B.C.E.	5%
2	Organization and Reorganization of Human Societies	600 B.C.E. to 600 C.E.	15%
3	Regional and Interregional Interactions	600 C.E. to 1450 C.E.	20%
4	Global Interactions	1450 C.E. to 1750 C.E.	20%
5	Industrialization and Global Integration	1750 C.E. to 1900 C.E.	20%
6	Accelerating Global Change and Realignments	1900 C.E. to the present	20%

Exam Structure

The AP World History exam is 3 hours and 15 minutes long. Section I is 1 hour and 35 minutes long and consists of 55 multiple-choice questions and 3 short-answer questions. Section II is 1 hour and 40 minutes long and consists of one document-based question (DBQ) and one long essay question (LEQ).

Section	Part	Percentage of Exam	Timing
I	Part A: Multiple-Choice (55 Questions)	40%	55 minutes
	Part B: Short-Answer (3 Questions)	20%	40 minutes
II	Part A: Document-Based (1 Question)	25%	100 minutes (includes a recommended 15-minute reading period)
	Part B: Long Essay (1 Question)	15%	

Question Types

Let's take a brief look at what question types you'll see on the exam. In the following chapter, we'll go into even more detail about how to approach each question type in order to earn a high score.

Multiple-Choice Questions

The 55 multiple-choice questions will be divided into sets of two to five questions based on a primary or secondary source, which could be a text excerpt, image, graph, or map. These questions assess your ability to understand and analyze historical texts and interpretations, as well as your ability to make larger historical connections. Keep in mind that even if a question set is based on a specific historical period, the individual questions may require you to make connections to other periods and events.

Short-Answer Questions

The three short-answer questions assess your ability to think like a historian by analyzing sources and interpretations, including text excerpts, images, graphs, or maps. In composing your answer, you do not need to develop and support a thesis statement, but you do need to synthesize your ideas into cohesive paragraphs. The short-answer section allows you to demonstrate what you know best since you get to choose what historical examples to discuss in relation to the prompts. Also, while two of the short-answer prompts are required, you will choose between two prompts for your final short-answer question.

Document-Based Questions

The document-based question (DBQ) assesses your ability to develop an argument based on your assessment of historical evidence. The documents on which this essay is based can vary in length and format, including written, quantitative, or visual materials. You are expected to make sophisticated connections based on the given documents; therefore, it is essential to demonstrate your knowledge of larger historical themes (rather than just events, dates, and people) in order to earn the highest scores.

Long Essay Questions

Like the document-based question, the long essay question (LEQ) also assesses your ability to develop an argument using historical evidence. This time, the emphasis is on explaining and analyzing significant issues in world history. In this section, you will answer one of three prompts, each of which focuses on different time periods. Make sure to choose the prompt that best show-cases the extent of your knowledge.

HOW THE EXAM IS SCORED

Once you complete your AP exam, it will be sent away to the College Board's AP Program for grading. The multiple-choice part is handled by a machine, while qualified AP graders—a group that includes history teachers and professors—score your essay responses. Your final score is a weighted combination of your multiple-choice and free-response section scores and is reported on a 5-point scale:

5 = Extremely well qualified

4 = Well qualified

3 = Qualified

2 = Possibly qualified

1 = No recommendation

"Qualified" means that you have proven yourself capable of doing the work of an introductory-level world history college course. Some colleges and universities will give you credit for a score of 3 or higher, but it's much safer to get a 4 or a 5. For specific rules regarding AP scores, check out each college's website or call their admissions office. If you do well on the AP exam, you may even get to move straight into a more advanced class (which is where the term "advanced placement" comes from)!

CHAPTER 2

How to Get the Score You Need

BOOK FEATURES

Kaplan's *AP World History Rapid Review* contains precisely the information you need to ace the exam. There's nothing extra in here to waste your time—no pointless review of material that's not on the exam and no rah-rah speeches. We simply offer the most potent test-preparation tools available.

Test-Taking Strategies

This chapter features an extended discussion of general test-taking strategies as well as strategies tailored specifically to the AP World History exam and the types of questions it contains.

Targeted Review and Practice

Chapters 3 through 7 cover all of the AP World History time periods and are designed to help you assess your current AP World History knowledge, as well as provide guidance on customizing your plan for studying.

Each chapter starts with the Test What You Already Know section, which includes two parts. Part A is a 10-question multiple-choice quiz, and Part B is a list of key topics you will check off if you can answer "yes" to at least three of the following questions:

- Can I describe this key topic?
- Can I discuss this key topic in the context of other events?
- Could I correctly answer a multiple-choice question about this key topic?
- Could I correctly answer a free-response question about this key topic?

After completing the Test What You Already Know section, you should then:

- review the quiz explanations in the back of the book
- read the Rapid Review section
- complete the Test What You Learned section and review the quiz explanations

The Rapid Review section includes a short time period summary as well as a brief definition for each key topic.

At the end of each Targeted Review and Practice chapter, the Test What You Learned section features a 10-question multiple-choice quiz as well as the same key topics checklist provided at the beginning of the chapter. You will be able to gauge your progress based on how much you have improved since you completed the Test What You Already Know activities.

STRATEGIES FOR EACH QUESTION TYPE

The AP World History exam can be challenging, but with the right strategic mindset, you can get yourself on track for earning the score you need to qualify for college credit or advanced placement. Before diving into strategies specific to the exam, let's review some general strategies that will aid you on any standardized test.

> ✔ **AP Expert Note**
>
> **General Test-Taking Strategies**
>
> 1. **Pacing.** Because many tests are timed, proper pacing allows someone to attempt every question in the time allotted. Poor pacing causes students to spend too much time on some questions to the point where they run out of time before completing all of the questions.
>
> 2. **Process of Elimination.** On every multiple-choice test you ever take, the answer is given to you. If you can eliminate answer choices you know are incorrect and only one choice remains, then that must be the correct answer.
>
> 3. **Knowing When to Guess.** The AP World History exam does not deduct points for wrong answers, while questions left unanswered receive zero points. That means you should always make an educated guess on a question you can't answer any other way.
>
> 4. **Taking the Right Approach.** Having the right mindset plays a large part in how well people do on a test. Those students who are nervous about the exam and hesitant to make guesses often fare much worse than students with an aggressive, confident attitude.

These points are generally valid for standardized tests, but they are broad in scope. The rest of this section will discuss how these general ideas can be modified to apply specifically to the AP World History exam. These specific strategies and the factual information reviewed in this book are the potent combination that will help you succeed on the exam.

Multiple-Choice Questions

The AP World History multiple-choice section consists of 55 questions, each with four answer choices, to be completed in 55 minutes. There is no penalty for incorrect answers, so guessing is encouraged. A primary or secondary document is provided for each question set, which will contain two to five questions. Question sets come from all six periods and can deal with specific countries and regions, global situations, or a single topic, such as the basic knowledge of a religion. Question sets are often comparative both within and across time frames.

The questions range from easy and medium to difficult with no distinct pattern to their appearance. A basic strategy for scoring well on this exam is to NOT do it linearly; in other words, do not take each question set one at a time, answering each one in order. The best strategy is to do the following:

- Answer all of the questions that you know and are sure about first.

- If you can eliminate at least two answer choices and the topic is familiar, mark the question by circling the question number in your exam booklet and move on.

- If you look at the question and do not remember the topic, mark the question with an X in your exam booklet and move on.

- Go back through the exam and answer the questions you marked with a circle. Try to eliminate at least two choices, then take your best educated guess as to the answer.

- Go back through the exam for a third time to answer the questions you marked with an X. Again, try to eliminate at least two choices, and take an educated guess.

Here are some more tips for doing well on the multiple-choice section:

- The easiest question may be the last one. Go through all of the exam questions!

- Move quickly but thoroughly through the exam. Don't linger on any one question for more than 30 seconds or so.

- If you skip a question, make sure that you skip that line on the answer grid.

- If you finish with time left, go back and check your answers, and make sure you have marked all responses correctly on the grid.

- DO NOT change an answer you have made unless you are absolutely sure that your initial attempt is incorrect. Research shows that your first answer is usually the correct one.

- When eliminating tempting wrong choices, look for choices that are out of the given time period or region or are not related to specific categories (e.g., the question asked for economic factors, and the answer choice mentions law codes).

Short-Answer Questions

On the AP World History exam, you have 40 minutes to answer three short-answer questions, each of which will have two to three parts. Aim to spend about 10 to 12 minutes on each question depending on how many parts it contains. Apply any extra time you have at the end of the section to reread your responses, looking for quick errors to fix (such as missing punctuation or wording).

Use the first minute to identify all of the parts of the question. Then, before you begin writing your answer, create a plan of which historical examples you will be using for each part. Your responses to each part should be between three and six sentences long.

Scoring

According to the College Board, a high-scoring short-answer question response will:

- *accomplish all tasks outlined in the question.*

- *use complete sentences.*

- *provide specific historical examples (going beyond simply quoting or paraphrasing to really explain an example's meaning or significance).*

Sample Short-Answer Question

Let's take a look at a sample short-answer question prompt.

Answer all parts of the question that follows.

(A)   Describe ONE reason that Mesopotamian city-states (3000 B.C.E. to 500 B.C.E.) were able to consolidate political power.

(B)   Describe ONE similarity in the socio-political structure of Mesopotamian city-states and the city-state of Athens (700 B.C.E. to 300 B.C.E.).

(C)   Explain ONE difference in the social or political structure of Mesopotamian city-states and the city-state of Athens.

As you can see, there are multiple parts of the prompt that your response will need to address in order for you to earn full credit.

Organizing Your Response

After reading the prompt, take a moment to jot down a few notes in the margin about how you plan to answer each part. For the short-answer questions, you should aim to write one to two paragraphs for each part of the prompt. You do not need to include a thesis for this question type, but you must use complete sentences; an outline or bulleted list alone is not acceptable.

Depending on the question, a high-scoring short-answer response may:

- explain a historical interpretation, compare two interpretations, and/or explain how evidence relates to an interpretation.

- address causes and effects, similarities and differences, or continuities and changes over time for different historical issues.

Using Historical Evidence

Even though short-answer responses do not need to be as complex as the responses for the document-based question or the long essay questions, they still require proper use of historical examples. Let's look at one way to successfully answer the last part of the sample question.

Explain ONE difference in the social or political structure of Mesopotamian city-states and the city-state of Athens.

> A difference between Athens and the Mesopotamian city-states is that Athens was a democracy and the Mesopotamian city-states were autocracies. Though previously ruled by individuals or groups of elites, Athens developed a system of direct democracy. Citizens attended the Assembly and voted directly on all matters. The Mesopotamian city-states, on the other hand, were ruled by powerful individuals who rose to prominence either by military conquest or through inheritance. Often claiming a divine authority, rulers could maintain their power through their coordinating of agricultural efforts, legitimization by the religious elites, and their control of the military.

Notice how this paragraph clearly answers the prompt, making sure to provide ample historical details. This response would not have received full credit if it had simply stated that Athens was a democracy while Mesopotamian city-states were autocracies. In this high-scoring response, the writer makes sure to insert specific information, citing the fact that Athenian citizens voted in the Assembly, and discussing the various ways Mesopotamian rulers justified and maintained their power. Short-answer responses like this one will help you conclude Section I of the AP exam with confidence.

The Document-Based Question

The first part of Section II is the document-based question (DBQ). This essay **asks you to think like a historian;** it will ask a specific question and present 7 related documents. Essentially, you are the historian who will take these sources and draw conclusions based on your analytical skills. The DBQ evaluates historical understanding at its purest: the task is not to remember facts but to organize information in an analytical manner.

If the DBQ prompt and accompanying documents cover something well outside the mainstream, don't panic! The exam writers do this on purpose. The other essay on the exam—the long essay question—will evaluate your knowledge of history, but the DBQ evaluates your ability to work with historical material, even material with which you're less familiar. Writing the DBQ is a skill that can be learned much like any other skill, and this book will help you hone that skill.

Organizing Your Response

The 100 minutes for Section II of the exam is divided into two parts: the first 15 minutes is the suggested reading and organizing time, and the last 85 minutes is the suggested essay writing time. The proctor will make timing announcements, and it is recommended that you spend 45 minutes writing the document-based question, and 40 minutes writing the long essay question. However, you will not be forced to move from reading to writing, or from the DBQ to the long essay, if you're not yet ready.

You will want to spend the first 10 minutes of the suggested reading period on the DBQ since this essay requires the most preparation time. Use the remaining five minutes to read and prep for the long essay question.

First, read the DBQ prompt. Underline the words that are most relevant to your task. Let's look at a sample question:

> Using the following documents, analyze how the Ottoman government viewed ethnic and religious groups within its empire for the period 1876–1908. Identify an additional document and explain how it would help you analyze the views of the Ottoman government.

All of the documents that follow will relate to the time period and the place, so you do not need to underline 1876–1908 or Ottoman government. You are being asked how the Ottoman government **viewed ethnic and religious groups** within its empire. An essay that dealt with how the groups viewed the Ottoman Empire would miss the point.

> ✔ **AP Expert Note**
>
> **Take a couple of seconds to read the instructions for the DBQ and each of the other essays. These list the tasks that you must accomplish to score well. Use these instructions as a checklist.**

Second, read the documents. Most of the first 10 minutes of the suggested reading period will be used to review the documents and organize them into groups for analysis. Each of the documents will have a number above a box. Inside the box will be information about the source of the document, which is very important as you will see later, and the document itself.

Documents can be of many different sorts. They can be pictures, photographs, maps, charts, graphs, or text. Written documents are usually excerpts of much longer pieces that have been edited specifically for the exam. They could be from personal letters, private journals, official decrees, public speeches, or propaganda posters. Obviously, the nature of the source should guide you in how you analyze the document. Often, students have a harder time analyzing the visual and graphic sources than the written sources. Even so, use all of the documents in your essay, treating the non-written sources with the same attention as the written ones.

All of the essay questions will be presented in a booklet. Feel free to write notes in this booklet as you read the documents and to underline important words in both the source line and the document itself. Nothing in the booklet is read as part of the essay scoring. Use the generous margins for notes that will help you group the documents together and discuss their points of view.

Jot down notes about the background of the authors in the margins. Information about the authors' social class, education, occupation, and gender may be important in the essay. At the bottom of the document, write a short phrase that summarizes the basic meaning of the document, its purpose (why it was written), and a missing piece of evidence that could relate to the document. If the document is a speech, the missing evidence could be the perception of those listening to the speech. If the document is a government declaration, the missing evidence could be information about how effectively the declaration was carried out.

It is also helpful to pause after reading all of the documents to consider evidence that would provide a more complete understanding of the issue. Then you can suggest an additional document.

> ✔ **AP Expert Note**
>
> **You will have to use black or blue ink to write your essays. If you are used to writing in pencil or typing, practice writing in ballpoint pen. Use a comfortable pen—one with a finger cushion and a wide diameter.**

Once you have finished reading and have made short notes of all of the documents, **reread the question.** Again, note what the question asks. If you have not done so already, mark which documents address the different issues that the question includes. Group the documents by their similarities. At this point, you should be able to draw enough conclusions to organize a strong, analytical thesis.

At the end of the 15 minutes, the proctor will announce that the time is up for the suggested reading period. If you have not yet finished reading and organizing your essays, take a few more minutes to finish up. A few students might be ready to write before the end of the reading period, but most find that the given time is just about right.

Scoring

According to the College Board, a high-scoring DBQ response will:

- *respond to the question with an evaluative thesis that makes a historically defensible claim. The thesis must consist of one or more sentences located in one place—either in the introduction or the conclusion. Neither the introduction nor the conclusion is necessarily limited to a single paragraph.*

- *describe a broader historical context immediately relevant to the question that relates the topic of the question to historical events, developments, or processes that occur before, during, or after the time frame of the question. This description should consist of more than merely a phrase or a reference.*

- *explain how at least one additional piece of specific historical evidence (beyond those found in the documents) relates to an argument about the question. This example must be different from the evidence used to earn credit for contextualization, and the explanation should consist of more than merely a phrase or a reference.*

- *use historical reasoning to explain relationships among the pieces of evidence provided in the response and how they corroborate, qualify, or modify the argument made in the thesis. In addition, a good response should utilize the content of at least six documents to support an argument based on the question.*

- *explain how the documents' point of view, purpose, historical situation, and/or audience is relevant to the argument for at least four of the documents.*

To effectively prepare for the DBQ, it is important to understand what components are needed for a high-scoring response. The AP World History exam readers will be looking for proficiency in four reporting categories: Thesis/Claim, Contextualization, Evidence, and Analyzing and Reasoning. The readers use a rubric similar to the following to determine your raw score, which can range from 0–7.

Reporting Category	Scoring Criteria	Decision Rules
Thesis/Claim (0–1 pt)	Responds to the prompt with a historically defensible thesis/claim that establishes a line of reasoning. **(1 pt)**	To earn this point, the thesis must make a claim that responds to the prompt rather than restating or rephrasing the prompt. The thesis must consist of one or more sentences located in one place, either in the introduction or the conclusion.
Contextualization (0–1 pt)	Describes a broader historical context relevant to the prompt. **(1 pt)**	To earn this point, the response must relate the topic of the prompt to broader historical events, developments, or processes that occur before, during, or continue after the time frame of the question. This point is not awarded for merely a phrase or reference.
Evidence (0–3 pts)	Evidence from the Documents: Uses the content of at least **three** documents to address the **topic** of the prompt. **(1 pt)** OR Supports an **argument** in response to the prompt using at least **six** documents. **(2 pts)**	To earn one point, the response must accurately describe — rather than simply quote — the content from at least three of the documents. To earn two points, the response must accurately describe — rather than simply quote — the content from at least six documents. In addition, the response must use the content of the documents to support an argument in response to the prompt.
	Evidence Beyond the Documents: Uses at least one additional piece of the specific historical evidence (beyond that found in the documents) relevant to an argument about the prompt. **(1 pt)**	To earn this point, the response must describe the evidence and must use more than a phrase or reference. This additional piece of evidence must be different from the evidence used to earn the point for contextualization.

(Continued)

Reporting Category	Scoring Criteria	Decision Rules
Analysis and Reasoning (0–2 pts)	For at least **three** documents, explains how or why the document's point of view, purpose, historical situation, and/or audience is relevant to an argument. **(1 pt)**	To earn this point, the response must explain how or why (rather than simply identifying) the document's point of view, purpose, historical situation, or audience is relevant to an argument about the prompt for each of the three documents sourced.
	Demonstrates a complex understanding of the historical development that is the focus of the prompt, using evidence to corroborate, qualify, or modify an argument that addresses the question. **(1 pt)**	A response may demonstrate a complex understanding in a variety of ways, such as: • Explaining nuance of an issue by analyzing multiple variables • Explaining both similarity and difference, or explaining both continuity and change, or explaining multiple causes, or explaining both cause and effect • Explaining relevant and insightful connections within and across periods • Confirming the validity of an argument by corroborating multiple perspectives across themes • Qualifying or modifying an argument by considering diverse or alternative views or evidence This understanding must be part of the argument, not merely a phrase or reference.

Sample Document-Based Question

Let's look at an example of a DBQ before learning how to earn the highest score possible.

> Using the following documents, analyze how the Ottoman government viewed ethnic and religious groups within its empire for the period 1876–1908. Identify an additional document and explain how it would help you analyze the views of the Ottoman Empire.

Document 1

Source: Adapted from Abdolonyme Ubicini and Pavet de Courteille, *The Present State of the Ottoman Empire*, a guide concerning the Ottoman Empire published in Western Europe, 1876.

FIGURES ON NATIONALITIES WITHIN THE OTTOMAN EMPIRE		
Ethnic Group (Total population) Percentage of Empire	**Subgroup**	**Subgroup Population**
Turkish group (14,020,000) 49.1%	Ottoman Turks	13,500,000
	Turkomans	300,000
	Tatars	220,000
Greco-Latin group (3,520,000) 12.3%	Greeks	2,100,000
	Kutzo-Vlachs	220,000
	Albanians	1,200,000
Slavic group (4,550,000) 15.9%	Serbo-Croatians	1,500,000
	Bulgarians	3,000,000
	Cossacks	32,000
	Lipovans	18,000
Persian group (3,620,000) 12.7%	Armenians	2,500,000
	Kurds	1,000,000
	Other Persians	120,000
Semites (1,611,000) 5.6%	Jews	158,000
	Arabs	1,000,000
	Other Semites	453,000
Other groups (1,232,000) 4.3%		
Total Population of the Ottoman Empire: 28,553,000		

Document 2

Source: The Ottoman Constitution, 23 December 1876.

Art. 1. The Ottoman Empire comprises present territory and possessions, and semidependent provinces. It forms an indivisible whole, from which no portion can be detached under any pretext whatever.

Art. 4. His Majesty the Sultan, under the title of "Supreme Caliph," is the protector of the Muslim religion. He is the sovereign and emperor of all the Ottomans.

Art. 8. All subjects of the empire are called Ottomans, without distinction, whatever faith they profess; the status of an Ottoman is acquired and lost according to conditions specified by law.

Art. 9. Every Ottoman enjoys personal liberty on condition of noninterfering with the liberty of others.

Art. 11. Islam is the state religion. But, while maintaining this principle, the state will protect the free exercise of faiths professed in the Empire, and uphold the religious privileges granted to various bodies, on condition of public order and morality not being interfered with.

Document 3

Source: Mr. Owen Davis, from a lecture at a British Congregational Church "Those Dear Turks," 1st November 1876.

Unfortunately for the peace of mankind, it has happened that the Turk is placed in a position where it is impossible to ignore him, and almost equally impossible to endure him; while by his origin, habits, and religion, he is an Asiatic of Asiatics, he is by irony of fate established in a position where his presence is a ceaseless cause of misery to millions of Christian people.

Document 4

Source: Hagop Mintzuri, an Armenian baker's apprentice, from his book *Istanbul Memoirs 1897–1940*, commenting about the military guards accompanying the sultan's arrival at a mosque for ceremonial prayers at the end of the fast of Ramadan.

First the Albanian guards, dressed in violet knee-breeches, who were not soldiers or police and did not speak Turkish, would fill the upper part of our market square. Then would come the Arab guards of the sultan, dressed in red salvar and adorned with green turbans. These too, did not speak Turkish and they would fill the road. Finally the Palace Guard of the sultan, chosen exclusively from Turks who were tall, sporting their decorations on their chests, would take up their positions as an inner ring in front of the Albanians and Arabs.

Document 5

Source: Süleyman Hüsnü Pasha (Pasha is a title of distinction within the Ottoman Empire), former high adviser to the sultan, commenting on the ethnic and religious diversity in Iraq, 7 April 1892.

The elements belonging to the official faith and language of the state are in a clear minority whereas the majority falls to the hordes of the opposition.

Document 6

Source: Ahmed Cevdet Pasha, respected Ottoman statesman and historian, undated official memorandum.

The Sublime State rests on four principles. That is to say, the ruler is Ottoman, the government is Turkish, the religion is Islam, and the capital is Istanbul. If any of these four principles were to be weakened, this would mean a weakening of one of the four pillars of the state structure. . . . The Sublime State is a great structure made up of various peoples and strata; all of these constituent elements are held together by the sacred power of the Caliphate. Because the only thing uniting Arab, Kurd, Albanian, and Bosnian is the unity of Islam. Yet, the real strength of the Sublime State lies with the Turks. It is an obligation of their national character and religion to sacrifice their lives for the House of Osman until the last one is destroyed. Therefore it is natural that they be accorded more worth than other peoples of the Sublime State.

Document 7

> Source: Proclamation by the Young Turks, 1908.
>
> 3. It will be demanded that all Ottoman subjects having completed their twentieth year, regardless of whether they possess property or fortune, shall have the right to vote.
>
> 9. Every citizen will enjoy complete liberty and equality, regardless of nationality or religion, and be submitted to the same obligations. All Ottomans, being equal before the law as regards rights and duties relative to the State, are eligible for government posts, according to their individual capacity and their education. Non-Muslims will be equally liable to the military law.

Crafting a Solid Thesis Statement

You have one chance to make a good first impression. Usually, an AP reader can tell within the first few sentences whether or not an essay is going to be strong. A few essays can recover after a poor start, but first impressions matter. Consequently, nothing is more important in the first paragraph than the clear statement of an analytical thesis.

Different kinds of writings demand different types of opening paragraphs. In English class, you may learn a style of essay writing that asks for general background information in a first paragraph. On a DBQ, however, you do not have much time. The reader is most interested in seeing a strong thesis as soon as possible.

Your thesis can be more than just one sentence. With the compound questions often asked by the DBQ, two sentences might be needed to complete the idea. To score well, the thesis needs to include specific information that responds to the question. Many students think they have written a thesis when, in actuality, they have not; their opening paragraphs are just too general and unspecific.

> ✔ **AP Expert Note**
>
> **Your thesis can be in the first or last paragraph of your essay, but it cannot be split between the two. Many times, your original thesis is too simple to gain the point. A good idea is to write a concluding paragraph that might extend your original thesis. Think of a way to restate your thesis, adding information from your analysis of the documents.**

The thesis is that part of your essay that 1) specifically addresses the terms of the question and 2) sets up the structure for the rest of your essay.

Let's take a look at thesis statement samples based on the prompt from earlier in the chapter.

> Analyze how the Ottoman government viewed ethnic and religious groups within its empire for the period 1876–1908.

Thesis Statements That Don't Work

The following statement is not an acceptable thesis; it is far too vague. It says very little about how the essay is structured.

> There were many ways in which the Ottoman government viewed ethnic and religious groups.

The next statement paraphrases the historical background and does not address the question. It would not receive credit for being a thesis.

> The Ottoman government brought reforms in the Constitution of 1876. The empire had a number of different groups of people living in it, including Christians and Muslims who did not practice the official form of Islam. By 1908 a new government was created by the Young Turks and the sultan was soon out of his job.

This next sentence gets the question backward: you are being asked for the government's view of religious and ethnic groups, not the groups' view of the government. Though the point-of-view issue is very important, this statement would not receive POV credit.

> People of different nationalities reacted differently to the Ottoman government depending on their religion.

The following paragraph says a great deal about history, but it does not address the substance of the question. It would not receive credit because of its irrelevancy.

> Throughout history, people around the world have struggled with the issue of political power and freedom. From the harbor of Boston during the first stages of the American Revolution to the plantations of Haiti during the struggle to end slavery, people have battled for power. Even in places like China with the Boxer Rebellion, people were responding against the issue of Westernization. Imperialism made the demand for change even more important, as European powers circled the globe and stretched their influences to the far reaches of the known world. In the Ottoman Empire too, people demanded change.

> ✔ **AP Expert Note**
>
> **Remember, if you ADD another paragraph or statement after writing a conclusion—that becomes your conclusion. Draw a line from any information added after the conclusion with an arrow to just before your conclusion. This keeps your conclusion valid.**

Thesis Statements That DO Work

Now we turn to thesis statements that do work. These two sentences address both the religious and ethnic aspects of the question. They describe *how* these groups were viewed.

> The Ottoman government took the same position on religious diversity as it did on ethnic diversity. Minorities were servants of the Ottoman Turks, and religious diversity was allowed as long as Islam remained supreme.

This statement answers the question in a different way but is equally successful.

> Government officials in the Ottoman Empire sent out the message that all people in the empire were equal regardless of religion or ethnicity, yet the reality was that the Turks and their version of Islam were superior.

Analyzing the Documents

The readers award credit based on what the essays accomplish. They do not remove points if an essay is off-task, written poorly, or wrong. There is one exception, however. In the DBQ, you must demonstrate that you understand the documents being used. If your essay makes more than one major misinterpretation, credit cannot be earned.

A major misinterpretation is one that misses the basic intent of the document. If you wrote that the Proclamation of the Young Turks (document 7) was a movement away from ethnic and religious equality, that misinterpretation would be a major error.

If, instead, you wrote that the Ottoman Empire survived for decades after the Proclamation of the Young Turks in 1908, the statement would be wrong (the Ottoman Empire collapsed after World War I) but would not be a misinterpretation of the document. All of the documents could still count as being understood properly. Be careful—especially with visual and graphic documents. Students tend to misinterpret these non-written documents more than they misinterpret traditional written documents.

> ✔ **AP Expert Note**
>
> **For charts and graphs, pay particular attention to the title and to the factors delineating the information in the visual. This will help you interpret the document. For pictures, remember that all pictures are taken for a reason and reflect the point of view of the photographer and/or the subject. Notice details in the background or foreground that can help you interpret them.**

Using Evidence to Support Your Thesis

Your ability to use the documents provided to answer the question is the focus of the essay. Use the documents to analyze, and you will earn credit for doing so.

If the essay supports the thesis with appropriate evidence from all, or all but one, of the documents, then the essay earns full credit. If it uses evidence from all but two of the documents, then partial credit is earned.

As you are writing your essay, check off each document in your booklet as you use it. When writing under the pressure of time, you may forget to mention one or two. Remember to include the documents that are in graphic or visual formats. Students often forget to analyze these to the same degree that they do written sources.

To receive full credit, the documents need to be used as part of the analysis. In other words, do you mention something about a document that helps to answer the question? If a document is mentioned only in a list, it will not count. For example, "The Ottoman Empire looked down on ethnic and religious minorities, as seen in documents 3, 4, and 5." If documents 3, 4, and 5 were not analyzed further, this essay would not receive full credit for supporting the thesis with appropriate evidence.

How should essays refer to the documents? Any of the following ways could count for supporting your thesis with evidence. Your essay could:

1. Refer to the document number directly in the sentence: "As shown by document 7, the Young Turks believed that all ethnic and religious groups should be treated equally."

2. Refer to the document within parentheses at the end of the sentence: "The Young Turks believed that all ethnic and religious groups should be treated equally (document 7)."

3. Refer to information presented in the line of source attribution: "As shown by The Proclamation of the Young Turks in 1908, the Young Turks believed that all ethnic and religious groups should be treated equally."

4. Combine the last two techniques: "As shown by The Proclamation of the Young Turks in 1908, the Young Turks believed that all ethnic and religious groups should be treated equally (document 7)." **(best option)**

5. Give no attribution: "The Young Turks believed that all ethnic and religious groups should be treated equally." **(worst option)**

Merely summarizing the documents is the easiest way to miss out on scoring well. You must link the document to the question, not just repeat what the document says. For example, the following paragraph might not count as evidence in support of the thesis:

> Document 1 is a chart with numbers for the different nationalities within the Ottoman Empire. Turks are 49.1% of the population. There are a lot of other groups listed too. The total population is about 28 million people. In document 2 the constitution says that the sultan is the religious authority and the sovereign. It also says that Islam is the state religion and that 'the state will protect the free exercise of faiths professed in the Empire, and uphold the religious privileges granted to various bodies.'

This summary does not provide any analysis. It states simply *what* the documents say; it does not describe *how* the documents show government views toward ethnic and religious groups. The task of the essay is to answer the question by analyzing.

The following paragraph would help earn full credit for evidence in support of the thesis:

> Document 1 is a chart that clearly demonstrates the ethnic diversity of the Ottoman Empire at the time of the new constitution. The Turks were a minority at 49.1% of the population, even though they controlled the government of the Ottoman Empire. The Constitution of 1876 (document 2) also reinforces the idea that the empire was formed of various ethnicities and religions. It formally states that all people are granted equality, and that all religions answer to the same law. However, this document reflects the law from the point of view of high government officials. It therefore demonstrates only the legal rules, rather than the day-to-day reality in the empire.

Another easy way to miss out on scoring well is by not having a strong thesis. How can you use document evidence to support the thesis if the thesis itself is weak? Your essay should be organized enough so that the reader can see how each document fits into the analysis presented in the thesis. Using the same terms that are mentioned in the thesis is a good way to make the links between the evidence and the thesis more apparent.

Discussing Point of View

Properly discussing the point of view (POV) of the documents is another important, and sometimes difficult, task. It separates the mediocre essays from those that score very well. Your essay will need to mention aspects of POV for at least two documents in order to receive POV credit.

So what is point of view? Essentially, POV is the analysis of why a certain person composed the material for the document. What is the author's (or the document's) "angle"? Comments in your essay that explore the motivations for the documents often count as POV. In addition, comments relating to the reliability of a source relate to that source's POV.

You cannot just say that an author is biased or prejudiced to receive the point for POV. You must state why or indicate an impact or desired effect of the document.

Ask these questions in order to earn the full credit for POV:

1. Does the occupation of the author give the document more or less reliability? For example, government officials may overstate or exaggerate information for political, state, or personal reasons.
2. Does the social class, religion, national background, or gender of the author influence what is mentioned in the document?

3. Does the type of document influence the content of what is said? A journal entry or private letter might be more candid about a topic than a public address that is meant to be persuasive. A political cartoon by definition is exaggerated and meant to convey a certain message, whereas a photograph may accurately represent what was in front of the camera for a shot, but could be staged and framed to capture only a certain perspective.

4. Does the timing of the document influence the message? Recollections and memoirs written long after an event may not have the same reliability as first-hand materials done immediately afterward.

5. Does the intended audience skew the message of a source? If a document is meant to be read by the sultan, it has a different POV than one written for a European audience.

6. Describing the tone of the document can also count for POV if the document is sarcastic, triumphant, haughty, etc. Using tone for POV can be more subtle and is best used with other descriptions of POV.

Merely attributing the document's source by repeating the source material from the document is not enough to earn the POV point. The source material, however, gives you clues as to what you could say relating to POV.

Using our sample DBQ on the Ottoman government's view of ethnic and religious groups, let's examine different examples of POV. You may want to go back to review the documents in the sample DBQ. The following statements may all count for point of view:

For document 1:

- "The census of national groups within the Ottoman Empire was compiled for Western European readers, which may make it more reliable in counting ethnic minorities than one published for a Turkish distribution." (intended audience and reliability)

- "The figures on nationalities provide a detailed picture of the population at the beginning of the sultan's reign but do not show how the population groups changed over time." (timing of the document)

- "The numbers in these census figures might be inexact because of the difficulty of counting widely dispersed people over a hundred years ago. The numbers seem rounded and may be educated guesses." (reliability)

For document 2:

- "The Constitution of 1876 reflects the official governmental laws and may not accurately represent the reality within the empire." (type of document)

- "The Constitution was most likely written by high government officials, who may have wanted the Ottoman Empire to seem more enlightened than it actually was." (background of the authorship)

- "The Constitution's protection of rights may have been an attempt to calm the masses during a sensitive time of transition." (timing)

For document 3:

- "Mr. Davis's speech may demonstrate anti-Muslim feelings that Europeans held at that time." (background of author and tone)
- "This speech given to a Christian group far away from the Ottoman Empire may be biased against the Ottoman government since the Ottomans were not in the mainstream of Western European society." (audience and reliability)
- "As a speech given in a British church, this document may have exaggerated the problems of the Ottoman government's treatment of Christians for dramatic effect." (type of document)

For document 4:

- "As an Armenian, Mintzuri was very aware of the different ethnic groups representing the sultan's guard." (background of the author)
- "Since this recollection was published in Mintzuri's memoirs years after the event, the details may be inexact." (type of document)
- "As a lower-class baker's apprentice, Mintzuri may have had strong feelings about his low position in society and consequently recorded the arrangement of guards as a ranking based on status." (occupation of author)

For document 5:

- "Süleyman Hüsnü Pasha, who had a title of distinction, was a former advisor to the sultan. Hüsnü's occupation had an effect on his opinion since he probably knew more about the conditions of the empire." (occupation of the author)
- "Since Süleyman Hüsnü Pasha was in political exile at the time of this document, he may have been more open about the situation in Iraq since he was not officially a part of the government." (background of the author)
- "Süleyman Hüsnü Pasha seems to hold a bias against the ethnic and religious minorities in Iraq, calling them 'hordes of the opposition.' This bias may have come from Hüsnü's loyalty to the official version of Islam and the Turkish language." (tone and background of author)

For document 6:

- "As a respected Ottoman statesman, Ahmed Cevdet Pasha was representing the official government views toward the different ethnic groups in the empire." (occupation of the author)
- "Since Cevdet's comments were in the form of an official memo, this document reveals the view of someone close to the power center of the Ottoman Empire." (type of document)
- "Most likely Ahmed Cevdet Pasha was a Turk and a Muslim and therefore would look more favorably on the role of Muslims and Turks within the Ottoman Empire." (background of author)

For document 7:

- "The Young Turks, as a revolutionary group of reformers, wanted the support of ethnic minorities. Consequently, they demanded complete liberty and equality in this proclamation to the people." (type of document, intended audience, and authorship)

- "The Young Turks wanted a new style of government. As a result they called on values different from those that had been practiced by the Ottoman officials." (background of authors)

- "Because this proclamation came in 1908 at the end of the sultan's rule, the message is more democratic and progressive than seen previously." (timing of document)

Some of the statements seem more sophisticated than others, and some of the statements may actually contradict each other. Even so, describing point of view is a skill that must be demonstrated for at least two documents.

Essays that use POV in a sophisticated manner and use it consistently are rewarded with very high scores, as long as every other basic component has been addressed.

Grouping Documents Together in Your Analysis

Historians analyze material by pulling together similar pieces of evidence, and, in writing your DBQ, so should you. The documents naturally come together into groups for analysis. Within each of your body paragraphs, group the documents. Essays that successfully have two or three groupings, depending on the question, often earn high scores.

Do not work with documents in isolation since a group cannot have just one document. A common mistake is for students to describe each document in order by paraphrasing what it says. This "listing" format is deadly to good performance on the DBQ.

Two earlier paragraphs served as examples of how to use and how not to use evidence to support your thesis. Let's look at these paragraphs again to see how effectively they group documents.

- "Document 1 is a chart with numbers for the different nationalities within the Ottoman Empire. Turks are 49.1% of the population. There are a lot of other groups listed too. The total population is about 28 million people. In document 2 the constitution says that the sultan is the religious authority and the sovereign. It also says that Islam is the state religion and that 'the state will protect the free exercise of faiths professed in the Empire, and uphold the religious privileges granted to various bodies.'"

- "Document 1 is a chart that clearly demonstrates the ethnic diversity of the Ottoman Empire at the time of the new constitution. The Turks were a minority at 49.1% of the population, even though they controlled the government of the Ottoman Empire. The Constitution of 1876 (document 2) also reinforces the idea that the empire was formed of various ethnicities and religions. It formally states that all people are granted equality, and that all religions answer to the same law. However, this document reflects the law from the point of view of high government officials. It therefore demonstrates only the legal rules, rather than the day-to-day reality in the empire."

In the first example, the documents are discussed independently. In the second example, they are discussed together, which creates a stronger paragraph.

Types of Groupings

How you group documents is a matter of personal opinion. Typical groupings include:

- chronological timing of the documents
- class, gender, occupation, and ethnicity of the documents' authors
- purpose or intended audience of the documents
- attitude and tone of the documents
- aspects covered by the documents (economic, political, social, or religious, etc.)
- geographic areas represented by the documents
- type of documents (pictures, charts, written documents, transcripts of speeches, etc.)

✔ **AP Expert Note**

Notice that a comparison is used to indicate that the documents are related and, thus, demonstrates a grouping. Using comparisons tells the reader that you are analyzing documents, not just listing them. Other ways to group your documents include by type, period, point of view, gender, social status, nationality, religion, location, and ideology.

For example, you could group the documents in the following ways:

By document type and intended audience:

- official proclamations/constitutions (documents 2 and 7)
- Ottoman internal correspondence (documents 5 and 6)
- documents intended for non-Ottoman audiences (documents 1 and 3)

By attitudes toward ethnic and religious minorities:

- documents that show inclusion (documents 2, 4, and 7)
- documents that show division (documents 3, 4, 5, and 6)

By focus on types of groups:

- documents that focus on religious groups (documents 2, 3, 5, 6, and 7)

- documents that focus on ethnic groups (documents 1, 4, 6, and 7)

You can group documents in a variety of ways. A single document can even be used in more than one group within an essay. You are encouraged to group documents in as many appropriate ways as possible.

Organizing Your Documents

A straightforward way to organize your grouping is to indicate why you are grouping documents together in your topic sentence. For example: "The Ottoman Constitution of 1876 (document 2) and the Proclamation of the Young Turks (document 7) both indicate that the Ottoman rulers wanted to ensure that all of their subjects understood that they were equal before the law. In the Ottoman Constitution, subjects are _____, while in the Proclamation of the Young Turks, subjects are _____."

Make sure to address each document when you list two or more documents in a grouping sentence. If you forget to actually use the document, it will cost you points for not using all of the listed documents.

Using Additional Historical Evidence

When doing research, historians continuously ask themselves where else they could find valuable information on a topic. Historians are in constant search of new areas of inquiry and new sources to explain the past. Since the DBQ is the essay that asks you to be a historian, your essay needs to provide suggestions for additional documents that could be useful in answering the question. These suggestions should not be types of documents that are already present in the DBQ, but rather the "missing voice" not already included in the list of documents.

For this task, you do not need to be very specific; you do not even need to mention a specific document. All you need to do is mention a type of document that could be useful in answering the question asked. The readers of the AP essay do not expect that high-school students would have knowledge of hidden documents in some archive that might shed light on this topic. General statements involving hypothetical types of documents would be fine *even if* they do not really exist.

Just as important as mentioning a potentially useful type of document is describing *why* it would be useful. To earn credit, you need to include both: mention of an additional document and an explanation about why it would be useful in analyzing the question. Unfortunately, students frequently mention a type of additional document without describing why.

For our sample DBQ, examples of additional documents could be:

- a document from the sultan himself since he represents the central power of the Ottoman Empire

- official orders from the Ottoman government on how to treat different ethnic and religious subjects since such a document could show how the government implemented its policies

- a chart showing statistics of religious diversity within the empire that would help describe the position of the official faith within the empire

- a speech or an article from a Young Turk on his attitude toward the Ottoman government that would help show the differences in thought between reformers and officials

- a document from a religious leader within the Ottoman Empire that would provide a sense of how official religious policies were perceived by the religious communities themselves

- a map showing the distribution of different ethnic groups within the Ottoman Empire, which would help illustrate the divisions faced by this multi-ethnic country

Any of these responses, or any combination of these, would receive credit as additional document(s). Other potential responses would also be counted if their importance could be explained.

Be careful: mentioning a type of document that you have already been given disqualifies the statement. For our sample DBQ, mentioning a document from a person outside of the Ottoman Empire would not count because document 3 is written from a British perspective. Nor would mentioning a document from an ethnic or religious minority within the Ottoman Empire count because document 4 is written by an Armenian in Istanbul. To make sure that you earn credit, you may want to mention two or three different types of additional documents and why each would be useful.

Students often mention an additional document at the end of the essay. However, discussion of the additional document can take place anywhere in the essay, and the most sophisticated essays will place this discussion of the additional documents as part of the body of the essay.

Going Beyond the Basic Requirements

Your goal for the DBQ is to earn the highest score possible. To earn a stellar score, several indicators of excellence may be considered. A high-scoring essay will likely:

- have a highly sophisticated thesis

- show deep analysis of the documents

- use documents persuasively in broad conceptual ways

- analyze point of view thoughtfully and consistently

- identify multiple additional documents with sophisticated explanations of their usefulness

- bring in relevant outside information beyond the historical background provided

Final Notes on How to Write the Document-Based Question

Do:

- Take notes in the margins during the reading period relating to the background of the speaker and his/her possible point of view.

- Assume that each document provides only a snapshot of the topic—just one perspective.

- Look for connections between documents for grouping.

- In the documents booklet, mark off documents that you use so that you do not forget to mention them.

- As you are writing, refer to the authorship of the documents, not just the document numbers.

- Mention additional documents and the reasons why they would help further analyze the question.

- Mark off each part of the instructions for the essay as you accomplish them.

- Use visual and graphic information in documents that are not text-based.

Don't:

- Repeat information from the historical background in your essay.

- Assume that the documents are universally valid rather than presenting a single perspective.

- Spend too much time on the DBQ rather than moving on to the other essay.

- Write the first paragraph before you have a clear idea of what your thesis will be.

- Ignore part of the question.

- Structure the essay with just one paragraph.

- Underline or highlight the thesis. (This may be done as an exercise for class, but it looks juvenile on the exam.)

The Long Essay Question

The long essay question (LEQ) on the AP World History exam assesses your ability to apply knowledge of history in a complex, analytical manner. In other words, you are expected to treat history and historical questions as a historian would. This process is called historiography—the skills and strategies historians use to analyze and interpret historical evidence to reach a conclusion. Thus, when writing an effective essay, you must be able to write a strong, clearly developed thesis and supply a substantial amount of relevant evidence to support your thesis.

Scoring

According to the College Board, a high-scoring long essay question response will:

- *respond to the question with an evaluative thesis that makes a historically defensible claim. The thesis must consist of one or more sentences located in one place—either in the introduction or the conclusion. Neither the introduction nor the conclusion is necessarily limited to a single paragraph.*

- *explain how a relevant historical context influenced the topic addressed in the question. It should also relate the topic of the question to broader historical events, developments, or processes that occur before, during, or after the time frame of the question. This explanation should consist of more than merely a phrase or a reference.*

- *use historical reasoning to explain relationships among the pieces of evidence provided in the response and how they corroborate, qualify, or modify the argument made in the thesis.*

The AP World History exam readers will be looking for proficiency in the same four reporting categories they use to assess your DBQ response: Thesis/Claim, Contextualization, Evidence, and Analyzing and Reasoning. The readers use a rubric similar to the following to determine your raw score, which can range from 0–6.

Reporting Category	Scoring Criteria	Decision Rules
Thesis/Claim (0–1 pt)	Responds to the prompt with a historically defensible thesis/claim that establishes a line of reasoning. **(1 pt)**	To earn this point, the thesis must make a claim that responds to the prompt rather than restating or rephrasing the prompt. The thesis must consist of one or more sentences located in one place, either in the introduction or the conclusion.
Contextualization (0–1 pt)	Describes a broader historical context relevant to the prompt. **(1 pt)**	To earn this point, the response must relate the topic of the prompt to broader historical events, developments, or processes that occur before, during, or continue after the time frame of the question. This point is not awarded for merely a phrase or reference.
Evidence (0–2 pts)	Provides specific examples of evidence relevant to the topic of the prompt. **(1 pt)** OR Supports an argument in response to the prompt using specific and relevant examples of evidence. **(2 pts)**	To earn one point, the response must identify specific historical examples of evidence relevant to the topic of the prompt. To earn two points the response must use specific historical evidence to support an argument in response to the prompt.
Analysis and Reasoning (0–2 pts)	Uses historical reasoning (e.g. comparison, causation, continuity and change over time) to frame or structure an argument that addresses the prompt. **(1 pt)** OR Demonstrates a complex understanding of the historical development that is the focus of the prompt, using evidence to corroborate, qualify, or modify an argument that addresses the question. **(2 pts)**	To earn the first point, the response must demonstrate the use of historical reasoning to frame or structure an argument, although the reasoning might be uneven or imbalanced. To earn the second point, the response must demonstrate a complex understanding. This can be accomplished in a variety of ways, such as: • Explaining nuance of an issue by analyzing multiple variables • Explaining both similarity and difference, or explaining both continuity and change, or explaining multiple causes, or explaining both causes and effects • Explaining relevant and insightful connections within and across periods • Confirming the validity of an argument by corroborating multiple perspectives across themes • Qualifying or modifying an argument by considering diverse or alternative views or evidence This understanding must be part of the argument, not merely a phrase or reference.

Success on the long essay section of the exam starts with breaking down the task of essay writing into specific steps.

Step 1: Dissect the Question

Always keep in mind that the AP World History exam is written to be challenging and rigorous. Thus, the questions will require you to identify specific and important information prior to constructing a response. When given an essay prompt, first take some of your time to slow down and understand exactly what the question is asking you to do. The key here is to understand how to answer all parts of the question. Circle directive words, such as *analyze, compare, contrast*, or *assess the extent to which*. Commonly, prompts will ask you to validate or refute a statement or to explain the impact of one event on another or the degree of impact. List these directives as pieces of the puzzle that you will attempt to put together with your history knowledge.

The following is a sample long essay prompt.

> Analyze the similarities and differences in the spread of Christianity and the spread of Islam between 100 C.E. and 1450 C.E.

✔ AP Expert Note

There Is No *U* In History

Don't include personal opinions in the essay. The reader is looking for your grasp of the history itself and your ability to write about it.

Step 2: Formulate a Thesis

A major area of concern each year for the AP exam readers is that students do not take the time to understand all parts of the question and plan their responses. Once you have dissected the question, it is time to plan a thesis. The thesis is your way of telling the reader why he or she should care about reading your essay. If you have a weak thesis, the reader will not be convinced that you understand the question. He or she will not trust that you have the depth of knowledge necessary to answer the question. Therefore, you must have a thesis that takes a stand, answers the entire question, and shows the reader the path you will take in your essay answer. It is not enough to merely restate the question as your thesis. One of the most important things to do is to take a position. Don't be afraid of taking a strong stand for or against a prompt as long as you can provide proper and relevant evidence to support your assertions.

✔ AP Expert Note

Think Ahead

During the planning time, make a short outline of all of the outside information you're planning to use in your essay; you will have the info handy while you're writing.

Think of your thesis as the "road map" to your essay. It will provide the reader with the stops along the way to the final destination—the conclusion. Only through a thorough study of world history can you construct a strong thesis.

Sample Thesis Statements

The following statement is not an acceptable thesis. It vaguely restates a portion of the prompt (that the spreads of the religions differed) rather than making a defensible claim. The mention of the Crusades is only a statement of fact, not a claim, and does not address the *spread* of the religions, which is what the prompt is really asking.

> Christianity and Islam differed in how they spread between 100 C.E. and 1450 C.E., but they came in contact with each other during the Crusades.

The next statement paraphrases the historical background and provides some specific details, but it does not address the entire question. It discusses the similarities of how Christianity and Islam spread, but it neglects to address the differences.

> Both Islam and Christianity began in the same world area, the modern-day Middle East, and each grew to become one of the world's major faiths. Christianity and Islam were similar in how they sometimes spread through force, leaders were influential in their spreads, and both religions split into two major branches during this time period.

Now we turn to a thesis statement that *does* work. This thesis is effective because it previews both the similarities (agents who spread the faith, divisions, and adoption by rulers) and differences (role of persecution and chronology of who spread the faith) as required by the essay prompt.

> Both Christianity and Islam were spread by missionaries and armies (though they differed in the chronology of this process), both experienced division, and both were adopted by rulers and impacted regional architecture. On the other hand, the spread of these two faiths differed in the roles of persecution and the chronology of the process of dissemination.

✔ **AP Expert Note**

Organize Your Writing Strategically

When composing your essay, start with your most important information. If you run out of time when you're writing, your key points are already in the essay.

Step 3: Plan Your Evidence

Now that you have a "road map," you need to brainstorm all of the relevant evidence you can recall that relates to the question. There are several ways to do this: a cluster or web diagram, a bulleted list, or a quick outline. Whatever you prefer, this is a step you *cannot* skip! Students who do not take the time to plan their evidence often find themselves scratching out irrelevant information during the exam, thus wasting valuable time. Also, you must learn to brainstorm efficiently—you should use only about five minutes to complete the first three steps of essay writing. Use abbreviations, pictures, or other cues that are efficient for you.

✔ **AP Expert Note**

Stick to the Subject

In your long essay, giving historical information before or after the time period in the essay topic will not get you any extra points.

Once you have a list, you can move to the next (and most important) step—writing!

Step 4: Write Your Essay

On the AP exam, time is of the essence! You will have 40 minutes to construct a coherent essay response for the LEQ if you use 60 minutes (including the 15-minute reading period) for the DBQ. If you practice the prewriting strategies from the previously outlined steps 1 through 3, you will find it easy to write a developed paper in a short time.

There is no "standard" number of paragraphs you must have. A good rule to keep in mind is one body paragraph for each portion of the essay prompt. Some AP World History exam questions will be structured to fit a five-paragraph essay, while others may need more and others less. You will not be penalized for writing a strong four-paragraph response. Likewise, you will not be rewarded for constructing a weak six-paragraph response. AP readers look for quality, not quantity.

Your first paragraph should always introduce your essay. Your thesis from step 2 is only part of your introduction. The first paragraph of your essay should include your thesis and any other organizational cues you can give your reader. Ask yourself, "Could a complete stranger understand where my essay is going from just my first paragraph?" If your answer is no, then you must rework the introduction. Do not spend time creating a "hook" or flashy statement for your first sentence. Do not use rhetorical questions. AP graders are reading for the items that are listed on the scoring guide. You will notice that creativity in language and structure is not a listed item. However, a well-written and developed argument is a desired item.

Your body paragraphs should follow the "road map" you set in your introduction and thesis. Don't stray from your plan, or you will find yourself straying from the question. You have taken the time to plan, so follow it! Do not merely list facts and events in a "laundry list" fashion. You must have some element of analysis between each set of evidence you provide. Using transition words, such as *however*, *therefore*, and *thus*, to show a shift in thought can make creating analytical sentences quick and easy. You should practice stringing facts and thoughts together using these "qualifying transitions" in your sentences.

> ✔ **AP Expert Note**
>
> **Know the Lingo**
>
> Whenever possible, use historical terms or phrases instead of general ones. For example, instead of saying that the South established laws against an owner freeing slaves, say that the South established laws against *manumission*. This shows the reader that you really know your stuff.

Beware of telling a story rather than answering the question. Readers are looking for analysis, not a revised version of your textbook. Do not attempt to shower the reader with extra factoids and showy language. Say what you need to say cleanly and simply. Readers will be impressed with your ability to write clearly and concisely in a way that showcases your historical knowledge, rather than your ability to write creatively.

Because this is a formal essay, you should avoid using personal pronouns, such as *you*, *I*, or *we*. Also, avoid the use of terms that could be "loaded" unless you intend on explaining them to the reader. For instance, you would not want to use the term *liberal* to describe Thomas Jefferson unless you were prepared to explain your use of the word *liberal* in the historical context. Do not use slang in any part of your essay. Because your essay is about history, write your essay in the past tense. Do not write about Franklin D. Roosevelt as if he were still alive today.

You should end each body paragraph with a "mini-conclusion" that ties the paragraph back to the thesis. It can serve as a transition sentence into the next paragraph or stand alone. In either case, the reader should be able to tell easily that you are shifting gears into another part of the essay.

Lastly, write your conclusion. Many students have learned that they should simply restate their thesis in the conclusion; these students may recopy what they wrote in the introduction word for word. This is incorrect. Yes, you should restate your thesis, but in a new way. Instead of rewriting it word for word, explain why your thesis is significant to the question. Do not introduce new evidence in your conclusion. The conclusion should tie all of the "mini-conclusion" sentences together and leave the reader with a sense of completion. If you are running out of time when you reach the conclusion, you may leave it off without incurring a specific penalty on the scoring guide. However, if you practice writing timed essays, you will learn the proper timing it takes to write a complete essay (conclusion included).

COUNTDOWN TO THE EXAM

Make Sure You're Registered

You can register for the exam by contacting your guidance counselor or AP coordinator. If your school doesn't administer the exam, contact the Advanced Placement Program for a list of schools in your area that do. Keep in mind that College Board's deadlines for registration are often at least two months before the actual exam.

There is a fee for taking AP exams, and the current cost can be found at the official exam website listed below. For students with acute financial need, the College Board offers a fee reduction that is usually equal to about one-third of the cost of the exam. In addition, most states offer exam subsidies to cover all or part of the remaining cost for eligible students.

For more information on all things AP, contact the Advanced Placement Program:

Phone: (888) 225-5427 or (212) 632-1780

Email: apstudents@info.collegeboard.org

Website: https://apstudent.collegeboard.org/home

Three Days Before the Exam

Practice answering exam-like questions. You can complete any quizzes you have not already taken in this book, or use practice resources on the College Board website. Use the techniques and strategies you've learned in this book. Approach exam questions strategically, actively, and confidently.

Two Days Before the Exam

Review the results of your exam-like practice. Don't agonize over whether you got a particular question right or wrong. The practice questions don't count; what's important is reviewing your performance with an eye for how you might get through each question faster and better on the exam to come.

> ✔ **AP Expert Note**
>
> **Don't just score your practice questions and move on! It's important to go over all of the answers and explanations, which can also serve as a quick review of important history material.**

The Night Before the Exam

DO NOT STUDY. Gather together an "AP World History Exam Kit" containing the following items:

- A few No. 2 pencils (Pencils with slightly dull points fill the ovals better; mechanical pencils are NOT permitted)
- Erasers
- A pen with black or dark blue ink (for the free-response questions)
- Your 6-digit school code (Home-schooled students will be provided with their state's or country's home-school code at the time of the exam)
- A watch (as long as it does not have internet access, have an alarm, or make noise)
- Photo ID card
- Your AP Student Pack
- If applicable, your Student Accommodation Letter, which verifies that you have been approved for a testing accommodation (such as braille or large-type exams)

Know exactly where you're going, how you're getting there, and how long it takes to get there. It's probably a good idea to visit your test center sometime before the day of the exam so that you know what the rooms are like, how the desks are set up, and so on.

Relax the night before the exam: read a book, take a hot shower, watch something you enjoy. Go to bed early to get a good night's sleep, and leave yourself extra time in the morning.

The Morning of the Exam

First, wake up on time. After that:

- Eat breakfast. Make it something substantial, but not anything too heavy or greasy.
- Don't drink a lot of caffeinated beverages, especially if you're not used to them. Bathroom breaks cut into your time, and too much caffeine is a bad idea in general.
- Dress in layers so that you can adjust to the temperature of the testing room.
- Read something. Warm up your brain with a newspaper, a magazine, or an online article. You shouldn't let the exam be the first thing you read that day.
- Be sure to get there early. Allow yourself extra time for traffic, mass transit delays, and/or detours.

During the Exam

Don't be shaken. If you find your confidence slipping, remind yourself how well you've prepared. You know the structure of the exam; you know the instructions; and you've had practice with—and have learned strategies for—every question type.

If something goes really wrong, don't panic. If you accidentally misgrid your answer page or put the answers in the wrong section, raise your hand and tell the proctor. He or she may be able to arrange for you to regrid your test after it's over when it won't cost you any time.

After the Exam

You might walk out of the AP World History exam thinking that you blew it. This is a normal reaction. Lots of people—even the highest scorers—feel that way. You tend to remember the questions that stumped you, not the ones that you knew. We're positive that you will have performed well and scored your best on the exam because you followed the Kaplan strategies. Be confident in your preparation, and celebrate the fact that the AP World History exam is soon to be a distant memory.

PART 2

Targeted Review and Practice

CHAPTER 3

Periods 1 and 2: Up to 600 C.E.

LEARNING OBJECTIVES

After studying these time periods, you will be able to:

- Describe the interrelationship between various societies and their environment.

- Describe cultural and technological diffusion resulting from interactions between cultures.

- Compare major world religions and belief systems.

- Explain how different governing forms are built and maintained over time.

- Describe how various societies' economic systems arise, and what they in turn cause.

- Describe the impact of environment and disease on migration and settlement.

- Explain how different governing forms are built and maintained over time.

- Explain the effects of society, culture, and environment on nation-states.

- Describe the impact of the environment on economic and industrial development.

CHAPTER OUTLINE

TIMELINE

Date	Region	Event
8000 B.C.E.	Mid East	Neolithic Revolution
5000 B.C.E.	Mid East	Sumer civilization in the Fertile Crescent
5000 B.C.E.	Africa	Agriculture begins in Nile River Valley
3500 B.C.E.	Mid East	Bronze Age
3000 B.C.E.	Africa	Pharaohs rule Egypt
3000 B.C.E.	Mid East	Indus River Valley civilization
1600 B.C.E.	East Asia	Huang He (Yellow River) civilization
550 B.C.E.	Mid East	Persian empire
600–501 B.C.E.	East Asia & South Asia	Buddhism, Confucianism, Daoism begin
500–401 B.C.E.	Europe	Greek Golden Age
403–221 B.C.E.	East Asia	Era of Warring States in China
321–185 B.C.E.	South Asia	Mauryan empire
221 B.C.E.	East Asia	Qin dynasty unifies China
32 C.E.	Mid East	Christianity begins
206–220 C.E.	East Asia	Han dynasty
320–550 C.E.	South Asia	Gupta Golden Age
476 C.E.	Europe	Fall of Rome
518–527 C.E.	Europe & Mid East	Justinian rules the Byzantine Empire

TEST WHAT YOU ALREADY KNOW

Part A: Quiz

Questions 1–3 refer to the map below.

ANCIENT RIVER VALLEY CIVILIZATIONS

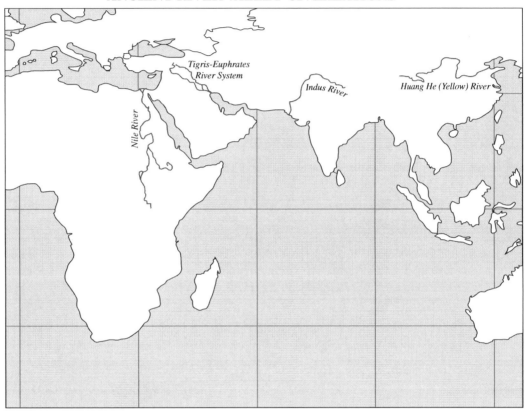

1. Which of the following correctly matches the river to the civilization that developed around it?

   (A) Nile: Indian civilization

   (B) Huang He (Yellow): Egyptian civilization

   (C) Tigris and Euphrates: Mesopotamian civilization

   (D) Indus: Chinese civilization

2. One society <u>differs</u> from the other three river valley civilizations pictured above in that it lacked

   (A) polytheistic religion

   (B) bronze tools and weapons

   (C) pictographic writing

   (D) social stratification

3. Which of the following statements correctly describes a consequence of establishing a society along a river?

   (A) In China, the annual flooding cycles were quite predictable.

   (B) In India, the Ganges River's proximity allowed civilization to spread.

   (C) In Mesopotamia, rivers confined trade to the Fertile Crescent.

   (D) In Egypt, the river served as a natural barrier against invaders.

Questions 4–5 refer to the map below.

MOHENJO-DARO AND HARAPPA

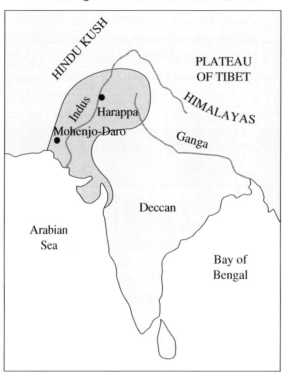

4. Mohenjo-Daro and Harappa were examples of

    (A) oasis towns along the Silk Road

    (B) dominant city-states in Ancient Greece

    (C) port cities along the Mediterranean

    (D) cities in the Indus River Valley

5. All of the following are featured at Mohenjo-Daro and Harappa <u>except</u> for

    (A) repositories of deciphered texts

    (B) streets and buildings laid out in grids

    (C) large public baths and sewer systems

    (D) expansive granaries for storing grain

Questions 6–8 refer to the passages below: Passage 1 is an excerpt from the Twelve Tables of Rome, circa 450 B.C.E., and Passage 2 is an excerpt from Hammurabi's Code, circa 1750 B.C.E.

Passage 1

"Table III.

1. One who has confessed a debt, or against whom judgment has been pronounced, shall have thirty days to pay it in. After that forcible seizure of his person is allowed. . . .

Table V.

1. Females should remain in guardianship even when they have attained their majority. . . .

Table VIII.

2. If one has maimed a limb and does not compromise with the injured person, let there be retaliation. If one has broken a bone of a freeman with his hand or with a cudgel, let him pay a penalty of three hundred coins. If he has broken the bone of a slave, let him have one hundred and fifty coins. If one is guilty of insult, the penalty shall be twenty-five coins.

3. If one is slain while committing theft by night, he is rightly slain."

Passage 2

"196. If a man put out the eye of another man, his eye shall be put out.

197. If he break another man's bone, his bone shall be broken.

198. If he put out the eye of a freed man, or break the bone of a freed man, he shall pay one gold mina."

6. The ideas expressed in the passages above most strongly represent which of the following historical trends?

   (A) The formal stratification of society

   (B) The development of religious morality

   (C) The idea that a republic's leaders were not above the law

   (D) An attempt to halt ongoing societal collapse

7. Which of the following did the Twelve Tables and Hammurabi's Code have in common?

   (A) Accusers could confront the accused in court.

   (B) Punishments were written to fit the crime.

   (C) Lower classes and higher classes were treated equally.

   (D) Men and women were treated equally.

8. Both of these documents were intended to

   (A) be flexible and change with the circumstances

   (B) protect the lower classes from the abuse of upper classes

   (C) provide democracy to their territories

   (D) unify the diverse customs of diverse populations

Questions 9–10 refer to the following religious texts: Passage 1 is an excerpt from the New Testament's Book of First Corinthians, Chapter 7; Passage 2 is a Buddhist poem translated by Thānissaro Bhikkhu, as written in the *Therigatha*.

Passage 1

"I would like you to be free from concern. An unmarried man is concerned about the Lord's affairs—how he can please the Lord. But a married man is concerned about the affairs of this world—how he can please his wife—and his interests are divided. An unmarried woman or virgin is concerned about the Lord's affairs: Her aim is to be devoted to the Lord in both body and spirit. But a married woman is concerned about the affairs of this world—how she can please her husband. I am saying this for your own good, not to restrict you, but that you may live in a right way in undivided devotion to the Lord."

Passage 2

"*Vimala: The Former Courtesan*

Intoxicated with my complexion,
figure, beauty, & fame;
haughty with youth,
I despised other women.
Adorning this body
embellished to delude foolish men,
I stood at the door to the brothel:
a hunter with snare laid out.
I showed off my ornaments,
and revealed many a private part.
I worked my manifold magic,
laughing out loud at the crowd.

Today, wrapped in a double cloak,
my head shaven,
having wandered for alms,
I sit at the foot of a tree
and attain the state of no-thought.
All ties—human & divine—have been cut.
Having cast off all effluents,
cooled am I, unbound."

9. Which of the following statements most accurately compares the role of women in Christianity and Buddhism?

    (A) In both religions, women could follow an alternative life in the monastery.

    (B) In both religions, men were considered spiritually superior.

    (C) Christianity attracted many female converts initially, while Buddhism attracted very few.

    (D) Buddhist women could not read sacred texts, but Christian women could read the Bible.

10. Which of the following is a similarity between Buddhism and Christianity?

    (A) Both religions have salvation as their ultimate goal.

    (B) Both religions are monotheistic in nature.

    (C) Both see their founders as fully human and fully divine.

    (D) Both had several variations early in their history.

Part B: Key Topics

The following is a list of the major people, places, and events for Periods 1 and 2: up to 600 C.E. You will very likely see many of these on the AP World History exam.

For each key topic, ask yourself the following questions:

- Can I describe this key topic?
- Can I discuss this key topic in the context of other events?
- Could I correctly answer a multiple-choice question about this key topic?
- Could I correctly answer a free-response question about this key topic?

Check off the key topics if you can answer "yes" to at least three of these questions.

Early Humans

- ☐ Animism
- ☐ Paleolithic

Development of Agriculture

- ☐ Job specialization
- ☐ Mesopotamia
- ☐ Metallurgy
- ☐ Neolithic Revolution

Development of Agriculture (cont.)

- ☐ Pastoralism
- ☐ Patriarchy

The First Civilizations

- ☐ Assyria
- ☐ Caste system
- ☐ Chavin
- ☐ Cuneiform

The First Civilizations (cont.)

- [ ] Egypt
- [ ] Hammurabi's Code
- [ ] Harappa and Mohenjo-Daro
- [ ] Hebrews
- [ ] Hinduism
- [ ] Mandate of Heaven
- [ ] Maya empire
- [ ] Olmecs
- [ ] Phoenicians
- [ ] Pictographs
- [ ] Qin dynasty
- [ ] Roman empire
- [ ] Shang
- [ ] Vedas
- [ ] Ziggurats

Classical Societies

- [ ] Alexander the Great
- [ ] Ashoka
- [ ] Christianity
- [ ] Daoism

Classical Societies (cont.)

- [ ] Diaspora
- [ ] Filial piety
- [ ] Gupta empire
- [ ] Han dynasty
- [ ] Hellenistic
- [ ] Indian Ocean trade
- [ ] Mauryan empire
- [ ] Monsoon winds
- [ ] Persia
- [ ] Phoenicia
- [ ] Republic
- [ ] Silk Road

Development and Spread of Religion

- [ ] Ancestor veneration
- [ ] Brahma
- [ ] Buddha
- [ ] Confucius
- [ ] Islam
- [ ] Shamanism
- [ ] Zoroastrianism

Tally Your Results For Part A and Part B

Part A: Check your answers and count the number of questions you got correct.

1.	C	6.	A
2.	A	7.	B
3.	D	8.	B
4.	D	9.	A
5.	A	10.	D

_____ out of 10 questions

Detailed explanations can be found in the back of the book.

Part B: Count the number of key topics you checked off.

_____ out of 50 key topics

Next Steps:

- Review the quiz explanations in the back of the book.
- Read the Rapid Review section.
- Complete the Test What You Learned section and review the quiz explanations.

RAPID REVIEW

Summary—Periods 1 and 2: Up to 600 C.E.

1. From the simplest barter system to long journeys along trade routes, the exchange of goods and ideas shaped this period and led to further change throughout the world. Important trade routes like the Silk Road, the Indian Ocean, and the Mediterranean Sea shaped development.

2. Once people began to settle and gradually organize into early civilizations, the discovery of agriculture began to change their lives at a more rapid pace.

3. As humans organized themselves in families, gender roles emerged. With the development of agriculture, the division of labor further deepened these divisions. These gender roles were reinforced by religious systems and governmental systems.

4. During this period, major world religions developed and spread, shaping the civilizations they encountered. Religions and belief systems, such as Hinduism, Buddhism, Confucianism, and Daoism (Asia), and Christianity and Judaism (Europe, Asia), influenced large numbers of people throughout the period.

5. Civilizations emerged that had organized governments, complex religions, social structures, job specialization, public works, systems of writing, and arts and architecture. These civilizations grew into larger and more complicated governmental organizations, such as empires (e.g., Rome, Han, and Gupta).

Key Topics—Periods 1 and 2: Up to 600 C.E.

Remember that the AP World History exam tests you on the depth of your knowledge, not just your ability to recall facts. While we have provided brief definitions here, you will need to know these terms in even more depth for the AP exam, including how terms connect to broader historical themes and understandings.

Early Humans

- **Animism:** Often found in primitive tribes, the belief that spirits can possess and control natural things and forces.

- **Paleolithic:** Literally, "old stone." The period from the appearance of the first hominids (human-like creatures) to approximately 8000 B.C.E.

Development of Agriculture

- **Job specialization:** As civilizations progressed and not everyone needed to farm to live, skilled laborers like artisans were allowed to craft things that had value. The trade that followed led to the growth of cities.

- **Mesopotamia:** Literally, "The Land Between the Rivers." Geographic region centered on the Tigris and Euphrates Rivers, located in modern-day Iraq. Considered one of the four major "cradles of civilization."

- **Metallurgy:** The crafting of metallic ores into functional and/or valuable items, beginning around 4500 B.C.E.

- **Neolithic Revolution:** Starting around 7000 B.C.E., this period marked the beginnings of permanent settlements and sedentary farming, leading to longer lives and higher populations.

- **Pastoralism:** The agricultural practice of domesticating animals for food or other uses, beginning around 4000 B.C.E.

- **Patriarchy:** A society in which men hold power within the family, in governance, and/or in economics.

The First Civilizations

- **Assyria:** Region in Southwest Asia spanning from modern-day Egypt to Iraq, this region was founded by a Semitic people around 2000 B.C.E. and lasted into the 600s B.C.E. Known for their fierce warrior spirit, the Assyrians were also great builders, creating cities like Nineveh and Ashur.

- **Caste system:** The system of social class division in Hinduism. From highest to lowest were the priests, warriors, skilled workers and free men, bonded serfs, and pariahs (untouchables).

- **Chavin:** Earliest known civilization in modern-day South America (c. 800 B.C.E.). Their mountain-based trade system helped the Andes Mountains become a cradle of Mesoamerican Civilization.

- **Cuneiform:** The Sumerian system of writing and one of the oldest forms of writing. Completed by pressing a wedge-shaped stylus into clay.

- **Egypt:** Located in Northeast Africa on the fringe of the Sahara Desert and centered on the Nile River, this nation is considered another one of the "cradles of civilization."

- **Hammurabi's Code:** Oldest known code of law. Issued by Hammurabi around 1800–1700 B.C.E. to unify his empire in Babylon, this code emphasized retaliation as punishment—"an eye for an eye, and a tooth for a tooth."

- **Harappa and Mohenjo-Daro:** The two key cities of the Indus River Valley Civilization. Located in modern-day Pakistan, they represent another one of the "cradles of civilization."

- **Hebrews:** Descendants of Abraham, considered the founder of Judaism, the first monotheistic religion. They settled in modern-day Israel c. 1500 B.C.E., then moved to Egypt.

- **Hinduism:** The majority religion of India today and the spiritual successor of Vedic thought. It emphasizes a cycle of reincarnation (rebirth), which can be improved or even broken by acquiring good karma for following the dharma, or rules, of one's caste.

- **Mandate of Heaven:** Ancient Chinese concept stating that the right to rule was granted by the heavens. Used to explain the rise of every Chinese dynasty from the Zhou in 1122 B.C.E. to the Qing in 1644 C.E.

- **Maya empire:** Peaking from about 250–900 C.E., the Maya empire, centered on the Yucatan Peninsula of modern-day Mexico, was known for its massive cities of Tikal and Chichen Itza. Trade in stone, shells, and cacao helped them thrive. Collapsed c. 900 C.E. under mysterious circumstances.

- **Olmecs:** Oldest known civilization in the Americas (c. 1000 B.C.E.). Centered in modern-day Mexico, they were known for their active trade, scientific developments, and giant stone heads.

- **Phoenicians:** Phoenicia was founded around 2000 B.C.E. in modern-day Lebanon, and this civilization based its livelihood on the sea. Skilled mariners, the Phoenicians traded their famed murex shells (used for "royal purple" dye) and red cedar trees. Their alphabet inspired the Greek alphabet. Collapsed around 600 B.C.E. with an Assyrian invasion.

- **Pictographs:** Many forms of ancient writing were based on symbols that represented a sound or a concept. Pictographic languages from this period include Egyptian hieroglyphics, Sumerian cuneiform, the text of the Harappan seals, and the text of the Chinese oracle bones.

- **Qin dynasty:** One of the earliest empires in Chinese history. From 221 to 206 B.C.E., the Qin dynasty was known for its use of iron and bronze, along with the beginning of the Great Wall.

- **Roman Empire:** The largest of the ancient world's empires, it stretched across the European continent and around the Mediterranean basin. Previously a republic, the empire was noted for its strong military, achievements in academics, and the spread of Christianity. Its peak was a 200-year period (about 20 B.C.E.–180 C.E.) known as the Pax Romana, or Roman Peace.

- **Shang:** A people speaking a Sino-Tibetan language, they developed an ancient civilization along the Huang He (Yellow) River in modern-day China. Along with Mesopotamia, South Asia, and Egypt, it is a "cradle of civilization."

- **Vedas:** A collection of hymns and chants, which would form the basis of Hinduism. The Vedas were some of the few artifacts left behind by the Aryans, nomads who took over the Indus Valley civilization c. 1500 B.C.E.

- **Ziggurats:** The hallmark of Sumerian architecture, these multitiered pyramids served as temples to the gods.

Classical Societies

- **Alexander the Great:** Macedonian king of the fourth century B.C.E. whose legendary conquests created an empire that included Greece, Persia, Southwest Asia, and parts of India. Responsible for the creation of Hellenistic culture.

- **Ashoka:** Great leader of the Mauryan Empire in India, he ruled around 250 B.C.E. Known for spreading Buddhism throughout India by sponsoring missionaries and encouraging vegetarianism.

- **Christianity:** Emerging in the first century C.E., this system of religion taught simplicity, love, compassion, and equality under one God. Based on the teachings of Jesus Christ, which are recorded in the New Testament. Quickly spread throughout the Mediterranean basin thanks to missionary activity, it is now the world's dominant religion.

- **Daoism:** Beliefs of Chinese philosopher Laozi (Lao Tsu), based on the Dao, or "the Way," in which people live in harmony with nature and believe in "less government."

- **Diaspora:** The mass spreading of the Ten Northern Tribes of Israel in 722 B.C.E., following an Assyrian invasion. This caused the loss of Hebrews' cultural identity. In the present, it can refer to the mass scattering of any group of people.

- **Filial piety:** Confucian virtue emphasizing respect toward one's elders.

- **Gupta Empire:** One of the first two empires of a unified India. The Gupta Dynasty (320–550 C.E.) revived Hinduism in India, delineated clear roles for men and women, and made great contributions in both the arts and sciences.

- **Han dynasty:** One of the earliest empires in Chinese history. From 206 B.C.E. to 220 C.E., the Han dynasty was known for its strong central government, thriving Silk Road trade, state-sponsored education, and general peace and prosperity.

- **Hellenistic:** Culture that fused the ideas of Greece and Persia, particularly after the conquests of Alexander the Great.

- **Indian Ocean trade:** Archaeological evidence confirms that Egyptians, Mesopotamians, Malays, Gupta Indians, and others utilized advanced marine innovations to trade valuable goods across the Indian Ocean.

- **Mauryan Empire:** One of the first two empires of a unified India. The Mauryan Dynasty (321–185 B.C.E.) saw the rise of Chandragupta and Ashoka, the spread of Buddhism, and a well-organized economy.

- **Monsoon winds:** Seasonal winds that affect weather patterns (and therefore, agriculture) in South Asia. Ancient mariners used these winds to carry them to India, allowing for a thriving trade throughout the Indian Ocean.

- **Persia:** Centered in modern-day Iran, they thrived around 500 B.C.E.–500 C.E. Their greatest kings, Cyrus, Darius, and Xerxes, helped expand the empire into Greece. In addition to being a great military power, Persia was remarkably well-managed, with its Royal Road.

- **Phoenicia:** Founded around 2000 B.C.E. in modern-day Lebanon, this civilization based its livelihood on the sea. Skilled mariners, the Phoenicians traded their famed murex shells (used for "royal purple" dye) and red cedar trees. Their alphabet inspired the Greek alphabet. Collapsed around 600 B.C.E. with an Assyrian invasion.

- **Republic:** First formed in Rome in 509 B.C.E., a government system in which the people elect their leaders and help create the laws. About 50 years later, the Twelve Tables helped to formalize Roman law.

- **Silk Road:** Network of land and sea routes facilitating trade between the Roman Empire, the Persian Empires, and the Chinese Empires. In addition to valuables, cultural ideas and new technologies traveled and spread along the routes.

Development and Spread of Religion

- **Ancestor veneration:** Often associated with the Chinese, this is the worship of the spirits of one's ancestors.

- **Brahma:** One of the three primary gods of Hinduism, he is regarded as the creator.

- **Buddha:** Born Siddhartha Gautama, this Indian prince founded Buddhism as an attempt to explain why there was suffering in the world. Buddhists today believe in the Four Noble Truths: that life contains suffering, that suffering is caused by desire, that desire can be rejected and nirvana (perfect peace) achieved, and that nirvana can be achieved through the Eightfold Path (a system of right forms of living).

- **Confucius:** Greatest of the Chinese philosophers (551–479 B.C.E.), his philosophy of reverence of ancestors, good education, and wise governance shaped the culture of China well into the twentieth century.

- **Islam:** The second most practiced religion in the world today. Founded in 622 C.E. by the Prophet Muhammad, it teaches the belief in Allah as the only god and Muhammad as the only prophet. A core tenet is the Five Pillars of Islam: declaration of faith, daily prayer, fasting during Ramadan, alms to the poor, and pilgrimage to Mecca (hajj).

- **Shamanism:** Often associated with indigenous tribes around the world, this system of belief involves a shaman, or spiritual medium, treating the ill by communicating with an unknown, unseen spirit world.

- **Zoroastrianism:** The religion of the Ancient Persians. Based on the teachings of Zoroaster in the Avesta, it teaches that life is a constant struggle of good versus evil in which good would always prevail.

TEST WHAT YOU LEARNED

Part A: Quiz

Questions 1–3 refer to the following passage.

"Popular usage defines 'civilization' along these lines: 'an advanced state of human society, in which a high level of culture, science, industry and government have been reached.' This definition is problematic for archeologists, anthropologists, and historians, because it contains an overt value judgment. . . .

Yet we know that some aspects of civilization seem in our judgment quite negative; large-scale warfare, slavery, coerced tribute, epidemic disease, and the subordination of women may come to mind. . . .

Serious students of archaeology, anthropology, and history use a technical definition of civilization that describes without conveying value judgments. Civilizations, in this technical sense, are a specific type of human community: large, complex societies based on domestication of plants, animals, and people, plus other typical characteristics. (Culture is everything about a human community, its knowledge, beliefs, and practices; civilizations are a particular kind of culture.)"

Excerpt from Cynthia Stokes Brown's "What Is a Civilization, Anyway?" 2009

1. Which of the following statements does <u>not</u> describe an important global development during the time period 8000 B.C.E. to 500 C.E.?

    (A) The formation of nomadic confederations led to an increase in trade along the Silk Road.

    (B) Metallurgy allowed people to make stronger and more efficient weapons and tools.

    (C) Systems of paper currency were developed in response to the growth in trade.

    (D) Writing developed in response to the need for record-keeping as civilizations developed and grew.

2. Which of these is an example of a civilization that collapsed internally?

    (A) The Phoenicians

    (B) The Minoans

    (C) The Gupta Empire

    (D) The Western Roman Empire

3. Which of the following <u>incorrectly</u> pairs a contribution to modern society with the location credited with its creation?

    (A) Direct democracy: Rome

    (B) Paper: China

    (C) Bronze: Mesopotamia

    (D) Solar calendar: Egypt

Questions 4–5 refer to the passage below.

"Chi K'ang asked how to cause the people to reverence their ruler, to be faithful to him, and to go on to nerve themselves to virtue. The Master said, 'Let him preside over them with gravity; then they will reverence him. Let him be final and kind to all; then they will be faithful to him. Let him advance the good and teach the incompetent; then they will eagerly seek to be virtuous.'"

Excerpt from Confucius' *The Analects*, circa 500 B.C.E.

4. Under Confucianism, all of the following are considered fundamental relationships <u>except</u> for

(A) parent and child

(B) husband and wife

(C) ruler and subject

(D) God and disciple

5. The social hierarchies of both Confucianism and Hinduism emphasized the value of

(A) peasants

(B) artisans

(C) government officials

(D) scholars

Questions 6–7 refer to the passage below.

"Beloved-of-the-Gods, King Piyadasi, speaks thus: To do good is difficult. One who does good first does something hard to do. I have done many good deeds, and, if my sons, grandsons and their descendants up to the end of the world act in like manner, they too will do much good. But whoever amongst them neglects this, they will do evil. Truly, it is easy to do evil.

In the past there were no Dhamma Mahamatras but such officers were appointed by me thirteen years after my coronation. Now they work among all religions for the establishment of Dhamma, for the promotion of Dhamma, and for the welfare and happiness of all who are devoted to Dhamma.... They work here, in outlying towns, in the women's quarters belonging to my brothers and sisters, and among my other relatives. They are occupied everywhere. These Dhamma Mahamatras are occupied in my domain among people devoted to Dhamma to determine who is devoted to Dhamma, who is established in Dhamma, and who is generous."

Excerpt from Ashoka's *Fourteen Rock Edicts*, circa 250 B.C.E.

6. The Mauryan Emperor Ashoka influenced the spread of

   (A) Sikhism

   (B) Hinduism

   (C) Zoroastrianism

   (D) Buddhism

7. Ashoka helped spread his religious policies in all of the following ways <u>except</u> for

   (A) encouraging vegetarianism and banning animal slaughtering

   (B) engraving edicts and building shrines throughout his empire

   (C) adapting the existing caste system to recognize middle castes

   (D) sponsoring missionary activity to the outer regions of his empire

Questions 8–10 refer to the passage below.

"The succession of emperors became a matter of dexterous manipulation designed to preserve the advantages of interested parties. The weakness of the throne can be judged from the fact that, of the 14 emperors of Dong Han, no less than 8 took the throne as boys aged between 100 days and 15 years."

"China," section on Han dynasty, *Encyclopaedia Britannica*

8. The Western Roman Empire's collapse had a greater negative effect in Europe than the Han dynasty's collapse had in China because

   (A) only Rome lost political control of its empire

   (B) continual waves of nomadic invasions made recovery difficult

   (C) the increase in Rome's population made feeding the population difficult

   (D) the Han dynasty in China was able to recover power

9. Which of the following can be inferred from the information about the ages of many Han emperors?

   (A) Influential parties at court were maneuvering young emperors to the throne while exercising real power in their name.

   (B) Han power grew when young emperors reigned, as the government was in the hands of capable regents.

   (C) The dynastic line was uninterrupted from father to son.

   (D) The Chinese people wanted a young emperor for religious reasons.

10. Which of the following Chinese imperial dynasties was overthrown by the Yellow Turban Rebellion?

   (A) Tang

   (B) Qin

   (C) Han

   (D) Sui

Part B: Key Topics

This key topics list is the same as the list in the Test What You Already Know section earlier in this chapter. Based on what you have now learned, ask yourself the following questions:

- Can I describe this key topic?
- Can I discuss this key topic in the context of other events?
- Could I correctly answer a multiple-choice question about this key topic?
- Could I correctly answer a free-response question about this key topic?

Check off the key topics if you can answer "yes" to at least three of these questions.

Early Humans

☐ Animism

☐ Paleolithic

Development of Agriculture

☐ Job specialization

☐ Mesopotamia

☐ Metallurgy

☐ Neolithic Revolution

☐ Pastoralism

☐ Patriarchy

The First Civilizations

☐ Assyria

☐ Caste system

☐ Chavin

☐ Cuneiform

☐ Egypt

☐ Hammurabi's Code

☐ Harappa and Mohenjo-Daro

☐ Hebrews

The First Civilizations (cont.)

☐ Hinduism

☐ Mandate of Heaven

☐ Maya empire

☐ Olmecs

☐ Phoenicians

☐ Pictographs

☐ Qin dynasty

☐ Roman Empire

☐ Shang

☐ Vedas

☐ Ziggurats

Classical Societies

☐ Alexander the Great

☐ Ashoka

☐ Christianity

☐ Daoism

☐ Diaspora

☐ Filial piety

☐ Gupta empire

Classical Societies (cont.)

- [ ] Han dynasty
- [ ] Hellenistic
- [ ] Indian Ocean trade
- [ ] Mauryan empire
- [ ] Monsoon winds
- [ ] Persia
- [ ] Phoenicia
- [ ] Republic
- [ ] Silk Road

Development and Spread of Religion

- [ ] Ancestor veneration
- [ ] Brahma
- [ ] Buddha
- [ ] Confucius
- [ ] Islam
- [ ] Shamanism
- [ ] Zoroastrianism

Tally Your Results for Part A and Part B

Part A: Check your answers and count the number of questions you got correct.

1. C   6. D

2. D   7. C

3. A   8. B

4. D   9. A

5. D   10. C

_____ out of 10 questions

Detailed explanations can be found in the back of the book.

Part B: Count the number of key topics you checked off.

_____ out of 50 key topics

Next Step: Compare your Test What You Already Know results to these Test What You Learned results to see how exam-ready you are for AP World History Periods 1 and 2: Up to 600 C.E.

CHAPTER 4

Period 3: 600 to 1450 C.E.

LEARNING OBJECTIVES

After studying this time period, you will be able to:

- Explain how states interact with peoples who do not identify with a state.

- Analyze the influence of politics on how states come into being, grow, and falter.

- Describe interactions between states and stateless societies.

- Describe the role of the arts in both changing and reflecting society.

- Describe the effects, both positive and negative, of legal systems and independence movements on race, class, and gender.

CHAPTER OUTLINE

TIMELINE

Date	Region	Event
570–632 C.E.	Mid East	Muhammad, founder of Islam
618–907 C.E.	East Asia	Tang Dynasty in China
711–1492 C.E.	Europe	Muslim occupation of Spain
750–1258 C.E.	Mid East	Abbasid Dynasty
750–1279 C.E.	East Asia	Song Dynasty in China
1096 C.E.	Mid East	First Crusade
1000–1200 C.E.	Africa	Kingdom of Ghana
1200–1400 C.E.	Africa	Empire of Mali
1211 C.E.	East Asia	Mongol conquests begin
1271–1295 C.E.	East Asia	Marco Polo's expeditions to China
1279–1368 C.E.	East Asia	Yuan Dynasty in China
1289 C.E.	Mid East	Ottoman Empire begins
1304–1369 C.E.	Africa	Ibn Battuta
1330 C.E.	East Asia	Bubonic plague
1368–1644 C.E.	East Asia	Ming Dynasty in China
1300–1600 C.E.	Africa	Kingdom of Kongo
1405–1433 C.E.	East Asia	Zheng He exploration in the Indian Ocean
1441 C.E.	Africa	Beginning of the Portuguese slave trade

TEST WHAT YOU ALREADY KNOW

Part A: Quiz

Questions 1–3 refer to the passage below.

"Genghis Khan ordained that the army should be organized in such a way that over ten men should beset one man and he is what we call a captain of ten; over ten of these should be placed one, named a captain of a hundred; at the head of ten captains of a hundred is placed a solider known as a captain of a thousand, and over ten captains of a thousand is one man, and the word they use for this number (is tuman). Two or three chiefs are in command of the whole army, yet in such a way that one holds the supreme command.

When they are in battle, if one or two or three or even more out of a group of ten run away, all are put to death; and if a whole group of ten flees, the rest of the group of a hundred are all put to death, if they do not flee too. In a word, unless they retreat in a body, all who take flight are put to death. Likewise if one or two or more go forward boldly to the fight, then the rest of the ten are put to death if they do not follow and, if one or more of the ten are captured, their companions are put to death if they do not rescue them."

Excerpt from Franciscan emissary John of Plano Carpini's letter to Pope Innocent IV, circa 1245 C.E.

1. Which of the following statements best describes the similarity between the impact of the Roman and Mongol empires?

    (A) They both brought all of Eurasia under one rule.

    (B) They both created a large economic market.

    (C) They both established large naval forces.

    (D) They both spread a common language.

2. Which of the following statements is true of the Turks and the Mongols?

    (A) Both conquered and ruled Korea.

    (B) Both were skilled administrators and bureaucrats.

    (C) Both had written languages based on Arabic.

    (D) Both were pastoral nomads originally from the Central Asian steppes.

3. The Mongol empire declined because of

    (A) religious differences with the native peoples

    (B) succession issues

    (C) feeble rulers after Genghis Khan

    (D) the Red Turban Rebellion

600 to 1450 C.E.

Questions 4–5 refer to the following passages.

"Kingdom of Mali

From the beginning of my coming to stay in Egypt I heard talk of the arrival of this sultan Musa on his Pilgrimage and found the Cairenes eager to recount what they had seen of the Africans' prodigal spending. I asked the emir Abu . . . and he told me of the opulence, manly virtues, and piety of his sultan. . . . Then he forwarded to the royal treasury many loads of unworked native gold and other valuables. I tried to persuade him to go up to the Citadel to meet the sultan, but he refused persistently saying: 'I came for the Pilgrimage and nothing else. I do not wish to mix anything else with my Pilgrimage.' . . .

This man [Mansa Musa] flooded Cairo with his benefactions. He left no court emir nor holder of a royal office without the gift of a load of gold. . . . They exchanged gold until they depressed its value in Egypt and caused its price to fall."

Al-Umari, circa 1324 C.E.

"Islam and Pilgrimage to Mecca

[T]he faithful . . . had the same objective to worship together at the most sacred shrine of Islam, the Kaaba in Mecca. One such traveler was Mansa Musa, Sultan of Mali in Western Africa. Mansa Musa had prepared carefully for the long journey he and his attendants would take. He was determined to travel not only for his own religious fulfillment, but also for recruiting teachers and leaders, so that his realms could learn more of the Prophet's teachings."

Mahmud Kati, *Chronicle of the Seeker,* circa 1330 C.E.

4. The sources about the travels of King Mansa Musa of Mali suggest which of the following about this West African kingdom?

   (A) Its centralized government made possible the development of an effective military.

   (B) Its people practiced diverse traditional religions and a nomadic agrarian economic system.

   (C) Its wealth came partly from gold resources, and the religion of Islam had spread to Mali.

   (D) Its wealth made possible the building of many mosques and a large university library.

5. After the expansion of Islam into West Africa,

   (A) the economy slowed

   (B) a decentralized government developed

   (C) civil war broke out

   (D) trade increased

Questions 6–8 refer to the passage below.

"[Novelist] Amin Maalouf . . . asks the question, 'Can we go so far as to claim that the Crusades marked the beginning of the rise of Western Europe—which would gradually come to dominate the world—and sounded the death knell of Arab civilization?'

[This is] a conclusion that is perfectly in keeping with the modern popular consensus in both the Middle East and the West. Popular it may be, yet it is nonetheless wrong. Scholars have long argued that the Crusades had no beneficial effect on Europe's economy. . . . Rather than decadent or 'assaulted on all sides' the Muslim world was growing to ever new heights of power and prosperity after the destruction of the crusader states in 1291. . . . Indeed, they are evidence of the decline of the Christian West, which was forced to mount these desperate expeditions to defend against ever expanding Muslim empires."

Thomas Madden, *The New Concise History of the Crusades,* 2005

6. Which of the following describes the major impact of the Crusades on Western Europe?

(A) European political dominance in the Levant aided their development of shipping technology.

(B) The exposure to Eastern goods and technology helped increase trade and foster a global outlook.

(C) The feudal system was strengthened as peasants encountered the cruelties of the West Asian labor systems.

(D) The failure of the Crusades set Western Europe back economically hundreds of years.

7. How did the Crusades most strongly affect the Byzantine Empire?

(A) Faced with Western hostility, the Byzantines made a temporary alliance with the Seljuk Turks.

(B) Aided by Western troops and financing, the empire retook much of Anatolia, Syria, and Jerusalem from the Muslims.

(C) They directly caused the Great Schism in Christianity, which isolated it in the face of later Turkish advances.

(D) Latin Christians were alienated from Western Europe, which isolated them in the face of later Turkish advances.

8. In the era of the Crusades, another instance of warfare leading to cultural transfers was

(A) the Columbian Exchange between the Western and Eastern hemispheres

(B) introduction of Christian thought to West Africa due to Portuguese and English conquests

(C) interchange of ideas and techniques between China and the Muslim world under the Mongol empire

(D) spread of Jewish philosophy and ritual to Prussia and Scandinavia during the Baltic Crusades

Questions 9–10 refer to the following map.

ZHENG HE'S VOYAGES

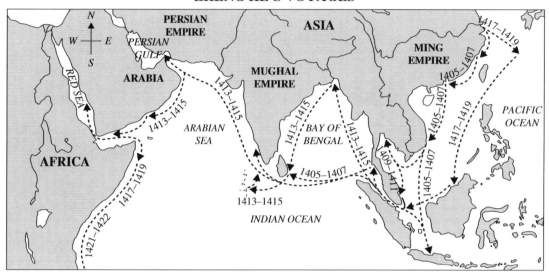

9. The map directly supports the statement that

    (A) the Ming made several voyages across the Indian Ocean

    (B) the Silk Route included a maritime path

    (C) Christopher Columbus and Ferdinand Magellan could not have accomplished what they did without East Asian navigators

    (D) the Chinese were already aware that the Philippines held nothing of value

10. Based on your knowledge of world history, the fears expressed in ending the voyages depicted on the map are best reflected in

    (A) Kublai Khan's conquest of China

    (B) the rise of the Umayyad dynasty

    (C) the sack of Constantinople

    (D) the downfall of the Mali Empire

Part B: Key Topics

The following is a list of the major people, places, and events for Period 3: 600 to 1450 C.E. You will very likely see many of these on the AP World History exam.

For each key topic, ask yourself the following questions:

- Can I describe this key topic?
- Can I discuss this key topic in the context of other events?
- Could I correctly answer a multiple-choice question about this key topic?
- Could I correctly answer a free-response question about this key topic?

Check off the key topics if you can answer "yes" to at least three of these questions.

"New" Empires

- ☐ Byzantine empire
- ☐ Islamic Caliphates

Chinese Empire

- ☐ Fast-ripening rice
- ☐ Grand Canal
- ☐ Neo-Confucianism

Korea

- ☐ Mongols

Islamic Caliphates

- ☐ Al-Andalus
- ☐ Astrolabe
- ☐ Mecca
- ☐ Muhammad
- ☐ Shi'a
- ☐ Sunni
- ☐ Trans-Saharan trade
- ☐ Umayyads

Decentralized States

- ☐ Charlemagne
- ☐ Feudalism

Western Europe and the Crusades

- ☐ Crusades

Europe during the High Middle Ages

- ☐ Bills of exchange
- ☐ Hanseatic League

Nomadic and Traveling Empires

- ☐ Polynesians
- ☐ Seljuk Turks
- ☐ Vikings

Mongols

- ☐ Genghis Khan

West African Kingdoms

- ☐ Bantu
- ☐ Mansa Musa
- ☐ Swahili city-states

Long-Distance Trade

- ☐ Melaka

Travelers

- ☐ Ibn Battuta
- ☐ Marco Polo

Spread of Disease

- ☐ Bubonic plague

European Developments

- ☐ Renaissance

Tally Your Results for Part A and Part B

Part A: Check your answers and count the number of questions you got correct.

1. B	6. B
2. D	7. D
3. B	8. C
4. C	9. A
5. D	10. D

_____ out of 10 questions

Detailed explanations can be found at the back of the book.

Part B: Count the number of key topics you checked off.

_____ out of 31 key topics

Next Steps:

- Review the quiz explanations in the back of the book.
- Read the Rapid Review section.
- Complete the Test What You Learned section and review the quiz explanations.

RAPID REVIEW

Summary—Period 3: 600 to 1450 C.E.

1. Similar to Periods 1 and 2 (up to 600 C.E.), Period 3 (600 to 1450 C.E.) witnessed a tremendous growth in long-distance trade due to improvements in technology. Trade through the Silk Road, the Indian Ocean, the Trans-Saharan routes, and the Mediterranean Sea led to the spread of ideas, religions, and technology.

2. Major technological developments such as the compass, improved shipbuilding technology, and gunpowder shaped the development of the world.

3. The movement of people greatly altered our world. Traveling groups such as the Turks, Mongols, and Vikings, for instance, interacted with settled people—often because of settled people's technology—leading to further change and development.

4. Religions such as Islam, Christianity, and Buddhism preached the equality of all believers in the eyes of God. And though patriarchal values continued to dominate, the monastic life of Buddhism and Christianity offered an alternative path for women.

5. The spread of religion, aided by the increase in trade, often acted as a unifying force, though it sometimes caused conflict. Christianity and the Church served as the centralizing force in Western Europe, and throughout East Asia, the spread of Confucianism and Buddhism solidified a cultural identity. The new religion of Islam created a new cultural world known as Dar al-Islam, which transcended political boundaries.

6. The political structures of many areas adapted and changed to the new conditions of the world. Centralized empires like the Byzantine Empire, the Arab Caliphates, and the Tang and Song dynasties built on the successful models of the past, while decentralized areas (Western Europe and Japan) developed political organization that more effectively dealt with their unique issues. The movements of the Mongols altered much of Asia's political structure for a time, and the recovery from the Mongol period introduced political structures that defined many areas for centuries to follow.

Key Topics—Period 3: 600 to 1450 C.E.

Remember that the AP World History exam tests you on the depth of your knowledge, not just your ability to recall facts. While we have provided brief definitions here, you will need to know these terms in even more depth for the AP exam, including how terms connect to broader historical themes and understandings.

"New" Empires

- **Byzantine empire:** Formerly the eastern half of the Roman Empire, this Christian (Eastern Orthodox) empire controlled the Eastern Mediterranean Basin from the Fall of Rome to the Ottoman takeover nearly 1,000 years later (474–1453 C.E.).

- **Islamic Caliphates:** In the Islamic world, the states controlled by caliphs, or successors of Muhammad.

Chinese Empire

- **Fast-ripening rice:** Introduced to China from Vietnam during the Tang Dynasty, this crop allowed the Chinese to have two harvests per year, dramatically improving output; combined with an improved infrastructure, this crop led to a significant growth of the Chinese population.

- **Grand Canal:** Begun in the fourth century B.C.E., construction resumed in 605 C.E. in China. This canal, the world's longest, connected the fertile Huang He River to the highly-populated cities in the north, allowing grain to be shipped easily.

- **Neo-Confucianism:** As trade expanded into China, Buddhism was introduced. Neo-Confucianism, popular during the Tang Dynasty, fused elements of Buddhism and Confucianism.

Korea

- **Mongols:** Group of Central Asian nomads from Mongolia who, under the leadership of Genghis Khan, conquered large portions of the Asian continent. Their four empires, centered on Russia, China, Persia, and the Central Asian steppes, were led by Khan's successors, ensuring a century of peace from approximately 1250–1350 C.E.

Islamic Caliphates

- **Al-Andalus:** Located in modern-day Spain, this Islamic state thrived in the 700s C.E. Led by the Berbers, this state was renowned for its achievements in science, mathematics, and trade.

- **Astrolabe:** Introduced to the Islamic world in the 700s C.E., where it was perfected by mathematicians. Used by astronomers and navigators to determine latitude through inclination.

- **Mecca:** Located in Saudi Arabia, it is considered the holiest city in Islam, as it is the birthplace of the Prophet Muhammad. A relic known as the Kaaba ("Black Stone") made it a pilgrimage site before the emergence of Islam. Today, it is the focal point of the hajj, a trip to Mecca that every Muslim must make during his or her lifetime.

- **Muhammad:** An Arabian merchant (570–632 C.E.) who, after a revelation from the archangel Gabriel, began preaching a new religion called Islam. His followers quickly spread the new faith throughout Arabia during the last 10 years of his life.

- **Shi'a:** One of the two main branches of Islam. Shi'a rejects the first three Sunni caliphs and regards Ali, the fourth caliph, as Muhammad's first true successor.

- **Sunni:** One of the two main branches of Islam, commonly described as orthodox, and differing from Shi'a in its understanding of the Sunnah and in its acceptance of the first three caliphs.

- **Trans-Saharan trade:** Starting in the 400s and 500s C.E., trade across North Africa thrived thanks to an organized network of camel caravans carrying gold, salt, cloth, slaves, and other valuables. This allowed the kingdoms of Ghana and Mali to thrive, and as Islam spread to Africa, allowed its teachings to impact the lives of kings and traders.

- **Umayyads:** Royal clan who took control of the first caliphate in 661 C.E. Their rule was hereditary. Under their rule, a dominant military rapidly expanded the empire, an efficient bureaucracy governed each territory, and subjected peoples were tolerated. The Umayyads' love of money, though, caused the Abbasids to overthrow them in 750 C.E.

Decentralized States

- **Charlemagne:** Ninth-century king of the Franks who ruled over the Holy Roman Empire. Despite his best efforts, his attempts to unify large territories failed, and the feudal system allowed lords and vassals to struggle for power.

- **Feudalism:** Developed in response to Viking invasions, this system allowed medieval Western Europeans to create a political system based on loyalty. A lord, usually a nobleman, would protect his vassal in exchange for mandatory labor or military service. In return, the vassal would receive a fief, or grant of land.

Western Europe and the Crusades

- **Crusades:** Launched by Pope Urban II in 1095 C.E., these holy wars were called in an attempt for Christians to reclaim the Holy Land of Israel from Muslim "infidels." The four campaigns, lasting over 100 years, were unsuccessful but did stimulate European-Muslim trade and reintroduce Europeans to wisdom that had been last taught during the Classical period.

Europe during the High Middle Ages

- **Bills of exchange:** Known as *sakk* in the Islamic world and also used in China during this period, these forerunners of modern-day bank checks were written guarantees of payment; these helped facilitate trade.

- **Hanseatic League:** Collaborative organization of trade guilds founded in Germany in the 1200s C.E., it dominated Northern European trade for the next two centuries.

Nomadic and Traveling Empires

- **Polynesians:** Indigenous to the distant islands of the Southwest Pacific Ocean, Polynesians used their geographic isolation to their advantage: they raised domesticated pigs and dogs, grew tropical fruit, and mastered seafaring to travel between islands.

- **Seljuk Turks:** Central Asian nomads who converted to Islam around the year 1000 C.E. By 1055, they had overtaken the Abbasid Empire, and they overtook the Byzantine Empire in 1071, laying the foundation for Muslim rule in modern-day Turkey.

- **Vikings:** Starting in the 800s C.E., these people from Scandinavia used their seafaring skill to terrorize Western Europe and settle in regions as far away as North America.

Mongols

- **Genghis Khan:** A Mongol clan leader who united the clans and made them the most feared force in Asia. Under his leadership, the Mongol Empire expanded greatly into China, Persia, Central Asia, and Tibet. His sons ruled the Four Khanates that followed, and his grandson, Kublai Khan, became leader of Yuan Dynasty China in 1279 C.E.

West African Kingdoms

- **Bantu:** Ancient peoples of West Africa who, starting around 2000 B.C.E., began a great migration to East and Central Africa. By encountering other Africans and Muslims, they adapted to their new surroundings and sustained their increasing population with the banana. Their language fused with Arabic to create Swahili, still spoken by many East Africans.

- **Mansa Musa:** Ruling from 1312 to 1337 C.E., he is the most famous of the Mali emperors. His capital, Timbuktu, was a center of trade, culture, and education. He is most famous, though, for going on hajj to Mecca (a practice that few Muslims in his time actually did) carrying a large caravan with satchels of gold, which he used to fund schools and mosques across his empire.

- **Swahili city-states:** As the Trans-Saharan trade dominated North and West Africa, East African trade was dominated by interchanges between Bantu and Arab mariners. Cities in present-day Somalia, Kenya, and Tanzania became bustling ports, and in an effort to facilitate trade, the Bantus created a hybrid language that allowed them to communicate with the Arabs. This language, Swahili, is still spoken by over 80 million East Africans.

Long-Distance Trade

- **Melaka:** Located in modern-day Malaysia, this port city became a way station for sea traders from China and India in the fourteenth century.

Travelers

- **Ibn Battuta:** Islamic traveler who, in the fourteenth century, visited the kingdom of Mansa Musa in the Mali Empire. His writings stimulated an interest in African trade.

- **Marco Polo:** Venetian merchant who spent over 20 years travelling the Silk Roads through the Mongol Empire, where he actually served on the court of its ruler, Kublai Khan. His efforts, which were compiled in a book, stimulated interest in trade with China.

Spread of Disease

- **Bubonic plague:** Also known as the Black Plague, this disease spread from China to Europe through rats. By decimating Europe's population, the plague ended the feudal system and led many to question religion.

European Developments

- **Renaissance:** Although Christian soldiers were unsuccessful in reclaiming the Holy Land, their exposure to Muslim advances in math, science, and the arts stimulated an interest in relearning classical wisdom. In an age when the unexplained was attributed to God, this caused people to begin questioning the true nature of phenomena, leading Europe out of the "Dark Ages" and into a period of artistic and scientific self-discovery, particularly from the fourteenth through the sixteenth centuries.

TEST WHAT YOU LEARNED

Part A: Quiz

Questions 1–2 refer to the following excerpt.

" . . . Another and perhaps more interesting issue is the obvious parallelism between what Buddhism and Islam imagined themselves to be: a cosmopolitan religion of the merchant elite. Both religions were therefore speaking to the issues and concerns of the same audience; and while such a situation may not be by definition untenable, in this case it turned out to be so and ultimately the 'Islamic international' beat out the 'Buddhist international.'

Islam was thus the first religion to be able to successfully challenge the entire support system that had sustained Buddhism for over a millennium. . . . At the ideological level it influenced the reinvestment of wealth in trading ventures by lay devotees; at the social level, donations to Buddhist monasteries provided status to traders; at the economic level, Buddhist monasteries were repositories of records and skills such as writing; and at the community level, participation in the fortnightly uposatha ceremony instilled an identity among the lay worshippers.

Islam with its prosperity theology, its mosques, and the larger networks of the Islamic community within the Caliphate clearly offered a viable alternative to all four of these structural components."

J. Elverskog, *Buddhism and Islam on the Silk Road*, 2010

1. Islam and Buddhism came into direct contact with each other during the time period 600 to 1450 C.E. in the region of

   (A) Western Europe

   (B) East Africa

   (C) Central Asia

   (D) Eastern Europe

2. What was the result of the cross-cultural exchange described by the historian in this passage?

   (A) A long-term tradition of hostility and competition between neighboring peoples

   (B) Borrowing of major elements of devotional practice and ritual over time

   (C) Synthesis and convergence between two world religions

   (D) Displacement of one ideology by another due to greater practicality or efficiency

Questions 3–6 refer to the following illustration.

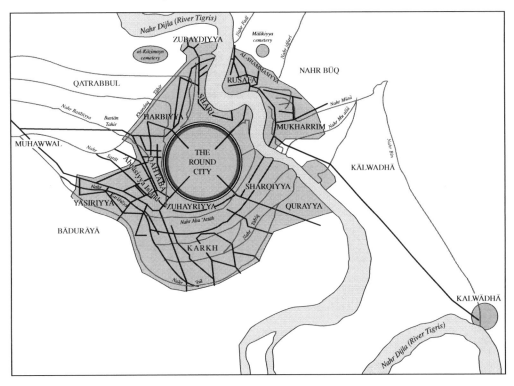

3. The city depicted in the map was an urban center along which of the following trade routes?

   (A) Mediterranean Sea

   (B) Silk Road

   (C) Trans-Saharan

   (D) Indian Ocean basin

4. The map suggests which aspect of commercial exchange between the years 600 C.E. and 1450 C.E.?

   (A) The Eastern Hemisphere was connected through both land routes and water routes.

   (B) Disease pathogens spread along trade routes, decreasing empires' populations.

   (C) Religious beliefs transformed as they diffused along trade routes.

   (D) Technologies such as printing and gunpowder were exchanged alongside goods.

5. Which of the following was the least significant consequence of commercial exchange in the city depicted in the map?

   (A) The spread of a plague

   (B) The introduction of porcelain

   (C) The writings of Marco Polo

   (D) The diffusion of Christian beliefs

6. All of the following facilitated commercial growth in the years 600 C.E. to 1450 C.E. except for

   (A) the minting of coins

   (B) government support of industry

   (C) the establishment of trade organizations

   (D) state-sponsored infrastructure projects

Questions 7–10 refer to the following excerpt.

"History is filled with the sound of silken slippers going downstairs and wooden shoes coming up."

Quote attributed to Voltaire, French Enlightenment writer, historian, and philosopher, circa 1740

7. The interpretation of history presented in the excerpt is best seen as evidence of which of the following events?

   (A) The establishment of the Kamakura shogunate

   (B) The rise of the Ghana Empire

   (C) The Red Turban Rebellion

   (D) The rise of the Byzantine Empire

8. Which of the following most directly resulted from Temujin's desire to prevent the downfall of the Mongol Empire after his death?

   (A) Dividing the conquered territory amongst his sons

   (B) The widespread adoption of Buddhism by the Mongols

   (C) Signing a peace treaty with Tang China

   (D) Establishing the *Pax Mongolica*

9. The view in the excerpt is most strongly reflected in which reform between the Han and Tang dynasties?

   (A) The military was deemphasized in favor of the tribute system.

   (B) The civil service examination was open to all males.

   (C) Higher-status women had more rights.

   (D) Neo-Confucianism was downplayed in favor of Buddhism.

10. Which of the following statements is an accurate comparison of the Mali and Mongol Empires?

    (A) Trade was discouraged in both the Mali and Mongol Empires.

    (B) The Mali collected taxes from their people, while the Mongols only demanded corvée.

    (C) The Mongol built their empire by conquering neighbors, while the Mali expanded their empire by sharing wealth.

    (D) Neither forced the conversion of their subjects.

Part B: Key Topics

This key topics list is the same as the list in the Test What You Already Know section earlier in this chapter. Based on what you have now learned, ask yourself the following questions:

- Can I describe this key topic?
- Can I discuss this key topic in the context of other events?
- Could I correctly answer a multiple-choice question about this key topic?
- Could I correctly answer a free-response question about this key topic?

Check off the key topics if you can answer "yes" to at least three of these questions.

"New" Empires

- ☐ Byzantine empire
- ☐ Islamic Caliphates

Chinese Empire

- ☐ Fast-ripening rice
- ☐ Grand Canal
- ☐ Neo-Confucianism

Korea

- ☐ Mongols

Islamic Caliphates

- ☐ Al-Andalus
- ☐ Astrolabe
- ☐ Mecca
- ☐ Muhammad
- ☐ Shi'a
- ☐ Sunni
- ☐ Trans-Saharan trade
- ☐ Umayyads

Decentralized States

- ☐ Charlemagne
- ☐ Feudalism

Western Europe and the Crusades

- ☐ Crusades

Europe during the High Middle Ages

- ☐ Bills of exchange
- ☐ Hanseatic League

Nomadic and Traveling Empires

- ☐ Polynesians
- ☐ Seljuk Turks
- ☐ Vikings

Mongols

- ☐ Genghis Khan

West African Kingdoms

☐ Bantu

☐ Mansa Musa

☐ Swahili city-states

Long-Distance Trade

☐ Melaka

Travelers

☐ Ibn Battuta

☐ Marco Polo

Spread of Disease

☐ Bubonic plague

European Developments

☐ Renaissance

Tally Your Results for Part A and Part B

Part A: Check your answers and count the number of questions you got correct.

1.	C	6.	B
2.	D	7.	C
3.	B	8.	A
4.	A	9.	B
5.	D	10.	D

_____ out of 10 questions

Part B: Count the number of key topics you checked off.

_____ out of 31 key topics

Next Step: Compare your Test What You Already Know results to these Test What You Learned results to see how exam-ready you are for AP World History Period 3: 600 to 1450 C.E.

CHAPTER 5

Period 4: 1450 to 1750 C.E.

LEARNING OBJECTIVES

After studying this time period, you will be able to:

- Describe the interrelationships between various economic exchange networks.

- Explain changes in the way governments work and are structured.

- Analyze the effects of labor reform movements, including changes in labor systems.

- Describe the impact of technological and scientific progress on populations.

- Describe the effect of exchange networks on culture across regions.

- Explain how industrialization and globalization were shaped by technology.

CHAPTER OUTLINE

TIMELINE

Date	Region	Event
1450 C.E.	Europe	Renaissance continues; Fall of Constantinople
1453 C.E.	Mid East	Ottomans capture Constantinople
1464 C.E.	Africa	Kingdom of Songhai is established
1492 C.E.	Americas	European explorers reach the New World
1517 C.E.	Europe	Protestant Reformation begins
1521 C.E.	Americas	Cortez defeats the Aztecs
1533 C.E.	Americas	Pizarro conquers the Inca
1588 C.E.	Europe	England defeats the Spanish Armada
1600 C.E.	East Asia	Beginning of Tokugawa shogunate
1618–1648 C.E.	Europe	Thirty Years' War between Protestants and Catholics
1652 C.E.	Africa	Cape Town Colony is established
1650–1800 C.E.	Europe	Enlightenment

1450 to 1750 C.E.

TEST WHAT YOU ALREADY KNOW

Part A: Quiz

Questions 1–2 refer to the image below.

WORLD SILVER TRADE: PRODUCTION, EXPORTS, AND IMPORTS

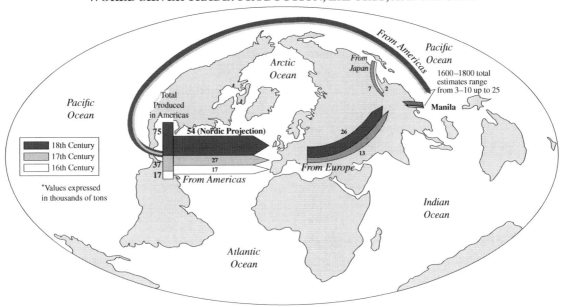

1. Which of the following statements most accurately describes the silver trade in the period from 1450 to 1750 C.E.?

   (A) Chinese demand for silver drove the trade.

   (B) Spain was unable to attain the needed supply of silver.

   (C) The Ottoman empire served as the middle-man in the trade.

   (D) The Ming dynasty was strengthened due to the inflation caused by silver.

2. What was one consequence of the silver trade in this period?

   (A) The Spanish empire used its great wealth to modernize its feudal economy.

   (B) A global trade system developed, the first between all major centers of civilization.

   (C) Britain waged the Opium War to force China off the silver standard.

   (D) Gold declined in value, increasing the volume of the Atlantic slave trade.

Questions 3–4 refer to the passage below.

"My Honourable Friends,

. . . For a Fort, at my first arrival I received it as very Necessary; but experience teaches me we are refused it to our advantage. If [the King] would offer me ten, I would not accept one. . . . the Charge is greater than the trade can bear; for to maintain a garrison will eat the Profit. It is not an hundred men can keep it; for the Portugal, if he once see you undertake that course, will set his rest upon it to supplant you. A war and traffic are incompatible. By my consent, you shall no way engage your selves but at sea, where you are like to gain as often as to lose. It is the beggaring of the Portugal, notwithstanding his many rich residences and territories, that he keeps soldiers that spends it; yet his garrisons are mean. He never Profited by the Indies, since he defended them. Observe this well. It hath been also the error of the Dutch, who seek Plantation here by the Sword. They turned a wonderful stock, they prowl in all Places, they Possess some of the best; yet their dead [fields] consume all the gain. Let this be received as a rule that if you will Profit, seek it at Sea, and in quiet trade; for without controversy it is an error to affect Garrisons and Land wars in India."

Excerpt from Sir Thomas Roe's letter to the East India Company, 1616

3. During the period 1450 to 1750 C.E., England rose as a dominant power in the Indian Ocean in part because

   (A) the English had defeated their major competitor, the Chinese, in the Opium War

   (B) it used joint-stock companies of private investors, who traded flexibly for profit rather than for royal prestige

   (C) the Ottoman empire had great difficulty retaining its position as the dominant power in the Indian Ocean

   (D) the Portuguese voluntarily withdrew their economic interests in the region

4. One consequence of the East India Company's monopoly of the India trade after the 1760s was

   (A) the American Revolution of 1776

   (B) Russian penetration of Central Asia in 1847

   (C) the Sepoy Mutiny of 1857

   (D) the settlement of Australia in 1788

Questions 5–6 refer to the passage below.

"Why, I asked, should we not admire the angels themselves and the beatific choirs more? At long last, however, I feel that I have come to some understanding of why man is the most fortunate of living things and, consequently, deserving of all admiration; of what may be the condition in the hierarchy of beings assigned to him, which draws upon him the envy, not of the brutes alone, but of the astral beings and of the very intelligences which dwell beyond the confines of the world. . . .

God the Father, the Mightiest Architect, had already raised, according to the precepts of His hidden wisdom, this world we see, the cosmic dwelling of divinity, a temple most august. He had already adorned the supercelestial region with Intelligences, infused the heavenly globes with the life of immortal souls and set the fermenting dung-heap of the inferior world teeming with every form of animal life. But when this work was done, the Divine Artificer still longed for some creature which might comprehend the meaning of so vast an achievement, which might be moved with love at its beauty and smitten with awe at its grandeur. When, consequently, all else had been completed (as both Moses and Timaeus testify), in the very last place, He bethought Himself of bringing forth man. Truth was, however, that there remained no archetype according to which He might fashion a new offspring, nor in His treasure-houses the wherewithal to endow a new son with a fitting inheritance, nor any place, among the seats of the universe, where this new creature might dispose himself to contemplate the world. All space was already filled; all things had been distributed in the highest, the middle and the lowest orders. Still, it was not in the nature of the power of the Father to fail in this last creative élan; nor was it in the nature of that supreme Wisdom to hesitate through lack of counsel in so crucial a matter; nor, finally, in the nature of His beneficent love to compel the creature destined to praise the divine generosity in all other things to find it wanting in himself."

Giovanni Pico della Mirandola, *Oration on the Dignity of Man*, 1486

5. Which of the following was one of the hallmarks of the Renaissance?

   (A) A new view of man as a creative and rational being

   (B) A celebration of Chinese and Islamic art and rejection of Greco-Roman styles

   (C) A declining interest in international travel

   (D) A growing acceptance of atheism

6. Which of the following describes a reason the Renaissance began in Italy?

   (A) Italian city-states were geographically isolated from most of Europe.

   (B) The Protestant Reformation weakened the Church's control over society.

   (C) Northern Italy helped supply and transport goods during the Crusades.

   (D) Political power in Italy was highly centralized.

Questions 7–8 refer to the image below.

Cortés Greets Xicotencatl, by indigenous Mexican artist, circa 1550

7. All of the following aspects of the Colombian Exchange are depicted in the above image <u>except</u> for

(A) novel methods of transportation

(B) military conquest

(C) political alliances

(D) disease pathogens

8. Based on your knowledge of world history, which of the following statements accurately describes an unusual aspect of the Aztec social structure?

(A) Its ruler claimed his authority derived from divine sources.

(B) Women could become property owners.

(C) In Aztec society, slavery was outlawed.

(D) Most Aztec commoners were artisans.

Questions 9–10 refer to the passage below.

"*Exclusion of the Portuguese, 1639*

1. The matter relating to the proscription of Christianity is known [to the Portuguese]. However, heretofore they have secretly transported those who are going to propagate that religion.

2. If those who believe in that religion band together in an attempt to do evil things, they must be subjected to punishment.

3. While those who believe in the preaching of padres are in hiding, there are incidents in which that country [Portugal] has sent gifts to them for their sustenance.

In view of the above, hereafter entry by the Portuguese *galeota* is forbidden. If they insist on coming [to Japan], the ships must be destroyed and anyone aboard those ships must be beheaded. We have received the above order and are thus transmitting it to you accordingly."

David John Lu, *Japan: A Documentary History*, 1997

9. What is an example of an early effort by a government to sustainably manage natural resources during the period 1450 to 1750 C.E.?

(A) The Tokugawa shogunate's laws to restrict timbering operations

(B) The British government's emissions restrictions to fight air pollution

(C) The Ottoman Empire's efforts to reduce overfishing in the Mediterranean region

(D) The United States' designation of protected lands such as Yellowstone National Park

10. Which of the following correctly describes Japan's foreign relations during the Tokugawa shogunate?

(A) The Tokugawa shogunate became more interested in expansionist policies resulting in the colonization of Korea.

(B) The Tokugawa shogunate implemented strict isolationist policies that halted all overseas trade routes entirely.

(C) The Tokugawa shogunate banned Christianity to prevent Spanish and Portuguese colonization attempts.

(D) The Tokugawa shogunate's contact with the West allowed for an influx of ideas and ushered in Japan's Industrial Revolution.

Part B: Key Topics

The following is a list of the major people, places, and events for Period 4: 1450 to 1750 C.E. You will very likely see many of these on the AP World History exam.

For each key topic, ask yourself the following questions:

- Can I describe this key topic?
- Can I discuss this key topic in the context of other events?
- Could I correctly answer a multiple-choice question about this key topic?
- Could I correctly answer a free-response question about this key topic?

Check off the key topics if you can answer "yes" to at least three of these questions.

European Exploration

- ☐ Caravel
- ☐ Columbus
- ☐ Conquest of Constantinople
- ☐ Ottoman

Trading-Post Empires

- ☐ Joint-stock companies

Columbian Exchange

- ☐ Columbian Exchange

Mercantilism: The Role and Impact of Silver

- ☐ Mercantilism

The Role and Impact of Sugar

- ☐ Sugar cultivation

State-Building

- ☐ Creoles
- ☐ *Daimyos*
- ☐ *Encomienda*
- ☐ Gunpowder
- ☐ *Haciendas*
- ☐ Manchu
- ☐ *Mestizos*
- ☐ Mughal empire
- ☐ Mulattos
- ☐ Peter the Great
- ☐ Songhai
- ☐ Tokugawa shogunate
- ☐ Triangular trade

Cultural and Intellectual Changes

- ☐ Printing press
- ☐ Protestant Reformation
- ☐ Scientific Revolution

The Environment

- ☐ Little Ice Age

Tally Your Results for Part A and Part B

Part A: Check your answers and count the number of questions you got correct.

1.	A	6.	C
2.	B	7.	D
3.	B	8.	B
4.	C	9.	A
5.	A	10.	C

_____ out of 10 questions

Detailed explanations can be found at the back of the book.

Part B: Count the number of key topics you checked off.

_____ out of 25 key topics

Next Steps:

- Review the quiz explanations in the back of the book.
- Read the Rapid Review section.
- Complete the Test What You Learned section and review the quiz explanations.

RAPID REVIEW

Summary—Period 4: 1450 to 1750 C.E.

1. As a result of the search for a faster way to the trade routes of the Indian Ocean, the Americas became part of the global trade network, and the process of true globalization began. This encounter set off the Columbian Exchange of goods, disease, and cultures, which spread throughout the world.

2. Improvements in and the spread of shipping technologies and gunpowder weapons allowed European countries to begin to exercise a more prominent role in world affairs.

3. Native American people died by the millions due to their exposure to previously unknown European diseases. African people were forcibly transported across the Atlantic Ocean to fill the need for forced labor on plantations.

4. New social structures emerged like those in the Americas based on race. While few women exerted power publicly, women of the harem in the Ottoman empire wielded considerable power behind the scenes.

5. In Europe, the Renaissance and Reformation challenged previously accepted beliefs and the power of the Roman Catholic Church. In other parts of the world such as China, the reaffirmation of more traditional beliefs was viewed as the key to stability.

6. European empires, such as Spain and Portugal, stretched their power overseas to conquer and control the newly encountered Americas. At the same time, dominant land-based empires such as the Ottoman, Mughal, and Qing grew powerful.

Key Topics—Period 4: 1450 to 1750 C.E.

Remember that the AP World History exam tests you on the depth of your knowledge, not just your ability to recall facts. While we have provided brief definitions here, you will need to know these terms in even more depth for the AP exam, including how terms connect to broader historical themes and understandings.

European Exploration

- **Caravel:** The ship of the European explorers during the Age of Exploration. Inspired by the Arab dhow, these compact ships of Portuguese origin featured triangular sails and a sternpost rudder, making them capable of crossing vast oceans.

- **Columbus:** Italian navigator who, under the sponsorship of Spain's Ferdinand and Isabella, attempted to sail a westward route to Asia. In so doing, his four voyages started a wave of Spanish colonization of the Americas and an exchange of new goods and ideas.

- **Conquest of Constantinople:** In 1453, the Byzantine Empire was brought to an end when the Ottomans conquered its capital in Constantinople (now Istanbul, Turkey) and converted its famous church, the Hagia Sophia, to a mosque. Muslim control of overland trade in the region gave Europeans the impetus to begin sea exploration at the end of the century.

- **Ottoman:** Group of Anatolian Turks who, in their dedication to Islam, attacked the weakening Byzantine Empire beginning in 1281. With their capture of Constantinople in 1453, this group created an empire in Southwest Asia and Southeast Europe until its collapse in 1923.

Trading-Post Empires

- **Joint-stock companies:** Predecessors of modern-day corporations, these large, investor-backed companies sponsored European exploration and colonization in the seventeenth and eighteenth centuries. One of the most famous ones was the British East India Company, which sponsored trade excursions to South and Southeast Asia.

Columbian Exchange

- **Columbian Exchange:** Beginning with the explorations of Columbus, this was the exchange of plants, animals, pathogens, and people between the Old World and the New World.

Mercantilism: The Role and Impact of Silver

- **Mercantilism:** The belief that one nation's power was based on its material wealth, particularly in gold and silver. This form of "economic nationalism" motivated European exploration.

The Role and Impact of Sugar

- **Sugar cultivation:** This land- and labor-intensive process was the impetus for the African slave trade, since diseases spread in the Columbian Exchange had decimated native populations. Further, the use of specialized labor and equipment was the predecessor of the First Industrial Revolution, which began by the year 1800 in the English textile industry.

State-Building

- *Creoles:* In the Spanish colonies, a term for a person of Spanish blood who was born in the Americas. Socially, they were second only to the *peninsulares*, those of Spanish blood who were born in Spain. Despite their relative wealth, they were treated as second-class. Consequently, the Creoles would serve as leaders of many of the independence revolts in South America in the nineteenth century.

- **_Daimyos_:** As feudalism was taking hold in Europe, a feudal system emerged in Japan. The system centered on the relationship between lord and warrior or peasant; the daimyo, or lord, controlled his land and his peasants. In exchange, the warriors, or samurai, provided protection. After a civil war in 1477, many of the _daimyos_ became rulers of their own tiny kingdoms.

- **_Encomienda_:** Spanish system of land grants that allowed colonists in the Americas to exploit the land and indigenous labor.

- **Gunpowder:** The first known chemical explosive. Created by the Chinese around 900 C.E., this chemical (and the weapons in which it was used) spread to the Islamic World and Europe via the Silk Road. In the fifteenth and sixteenth centuries, Europeans perfected the manufacture of a slow-burning propellant to maximize the potential of explosive-based weapons.

- **_Haciendas_:** Spanish system of landed estates. Originally, these were government-granted and allowed the use of exploited labor. Over time, though, the Spanish Crown phased out the _encomienda_ system, allowing private ownership and free recruitment of labor. This system continued into the twentieth century.

- **Manchu:** A nomadic group from Northeast China, they were the principal rulers of the Qing Dynasty, which saw a drastically increasing population and agricultural innovation, along with foreign intervention. The Qing was the last Chinese dynasty, lasting from 1644 to 1912 C.E.

- **_Mestizos_ and _mulattos_:** Terms for new mixed races that emerged in the Americas in the wake of colonization. _Mestizos_ were half European and half Native American, while _mulattos_ were half European and half African. Both were treated as lower class.

- **Mughal empire:** Islamic empire that reunified India in 1526 under Babur. His grandson, Akbar, advocated religious tolerance and sponsored great art and architecture projects. Under Aurangzeb, however, the large kingdom collapsed due to discord between Muslims and Hindus.

- **Peter the Great:** Tsar of Russia from 1682 to 1725. His fascination with Western arts and sciences led him to rapidly modernize Russia under autocratic rule. The city of St. Petersburg, which was designed in a grid pattern like a Western European city, is named for and was built by him.

- **Songhai:** Successor of the great Mali Empire in West Africa, this empire thrived for over 100 years in the fifteenth and sixteenth centuries, thanks to the capable leadership, bureaucracy, and military of Emperor Sunni Ali.

- **Tokugawa shogunate:** Ruling Japan from 1600 to 1867, this was a period of relative stability. Under Tokugawa Ieyasu and his successors, the daimyo had less power, and Western Christian merchants were forbidden from doing any trade, with the exception of the Dutch, who weren't interested in spreading Christianity.

- **Triangular trade:** As Europeans began colonizing the Caribbean Islands and other tropical regions of the Americas, a complex trading network emerged: Europeans exchanged their manufactured goods with Africans, who exchanged their slaves with the American colonists, who exchanged their tropical crops (including sugar and its byproducts, rum and molasses) with Europeans.

Cultural and Intellectual Changes

- **Printing press:** Although movable type had been used in China since at least 1100 C.E., Johannes Gutenberg of Germany perfected the printing press and made mass printing possible in Europe in 1456. Due to the relative cheapness of printing books, knowledge and literacy became more accessible to the masses. For this reason, some historians consider it the greatest invention of the past millennium.

- **Protestant Reformation:** As the Catholic Church grew more powerful in Europe, people began to question its true authority, especially with the humanistic spirit of the Renaissance. In response to the corrupt practice of indulgences ("selling salvation"), Martin Luther, an excommunicated priest, traveled around Germany sharing a simple message that "the just shall live by faith alone." His words inspired other Protestant reformers, including John Calvin and John Wesley.

- **Scientific Revolution:** A product of both Renaissance and Enlightenment thinking, this was a period of scientific observation and exploration in which people attempted to explain what was previously unexplainable or attributed to God. Although its proponents, including Copernicus and Galileo, taught things that directly went against Church doctrine, their work inspired the modern scientific method.

The Environment

- **Little Ice Age:** Climatic period of cooling from the fourteenth through the nineteenth centuries in the Northern Hemisphere. In Europe, this devastated farms close to mountain glaciers, causing frequent famines. In North America, this caused the collapse of Norse settlements by isolating them from other mainland territories, due to increased storm activity and ocean ice.

1450 to 1750 C.E.

TEST WHAT YOU LEARNED

Part A: Quiz

Questions 1–2 refer to the passage below.

"*The Status of Jews and Christians in Muslim Lands*

What do you say, O scholars of Islam, shining luminaries who dispel the darkness (may God lengthen your days!)? What do you say of the innovations introduced by the cursed unbelievers [Jewish and Christian] into Cairo, into the city of al-Muizz [founder of Cairo, 969] which by its splendor in legal and philosophic studies sparkles in the first rank of Muslim cities?

Ought one to allow these things to the unbelievers, to the enemies of the faith? Ought one to allow them to dwell among believers under such conditions? Or, indeed, is it not the duty of every Muslim prince and of every magistrate to ask the scholars of the holy law to express their legal opinion, and to call for the advice of wise and enlightened men in order to put an end to these revolting innovations and to these reprehensible acts? Ought one not compel the unbelievers to stick to their pact [of Umar]; ought one not keep them in servitude and prevent them from going beyond the bounds and the limits of their tolerated status in order that there may result from this the greatest glory of God, of His Prophet, and of all Muslims, and likewise of that which is said in the Qu'ran?"

Jacob Marcus, *The Jew in the Medieval World: A Sourcebook, 315–1791,* 1938

1. The Ottoman, Safavid, and Mughal empires had all of the following in common <u>except</u>

   (A) utilization of firearms

   (B) political support of Islam

   (C) artistic innovations and achievements

   (D) economic dependence on oil

2. Which of the following is a difference between the early Islamic empires (1450–1750 C.E.)?

   (A) Only the Mughal empire contained a substantial number of non-Muslims.

   (B) The Ottoman empire was mostly Sunni while the Safavid was mostly Shi'ite.

   (C) Only the Ottoman empire had a military-based society.

   (D) Not all experienced problems of succession from one ruler to the next.

Questions 3–4 refer to the passage below.

"Yesterday your ambassador petitioned my ministers to memorialize me regarding your trade with China, but his proposal is not consistent with our dynastic usage and cannot be entertained. Hitherto, all European nations, including your own country's barbarian merchants, have carried on their trade with our Celestial Empire at Guangzhou. Such has been the procedure for many years, although our Celestial Empire possesses all things in prolific abundance and lacks no product within its own borders. There was therefore no need to import the manufactures of outside barbarians in exchange for our own produce."

Excerpt from a letter Chinese emperor Qianlong wrote to King George III of England, 1793

3. Which of the following regions was <u>least</u> affected by maritime reconnaissance voyages in the period 1450–1750 C.E.?

   (A) The Indian Ocean region

   (B) West Africa

   (C) South America

   (D) Oceania and Polynesia

4. All of the following are reasons why China stopped its global exploration during the fifteenth century <u>except</u> for

   (A) political leaders fearing an influx of new technological innovations would lead to social instability

   (B) Confucian values denouncing mercantilism and instead stressing the importance of frugality over expensive voyages

   (C) threats of Mongol invasions forcing rulers to concentrate attention and resources on the country's borders

   (D) rulers fearing colonization by the European empires and wanting to ensure China's safety and sovereignty

Questions 5–6 refer to the passage below.

"With the successive losses of two Ming capitals [to the invading Qing], locally prominent families and minor officials in Kiangnan had been sorely pressed to contain a rash of uprisings by various discontented and lawless elements—mainly tenants, indentured persons, and underground groups—and they now welcomed any authority that could restore the social order to which they were accustomed. Consequently, the first appearance of Han Chinese Qing officials in most locales was relatively uneventful, as social leaders adopted a cooperative, wait-and-see attitude. However, . . . it became clearer that 'barbarians' were really in charge, a common cause to oppose the Qing was forged among social elements that otherwise would have been at odds."

Excerpt from L. A. Struve's *The Southern Ming, 1644–1662*, 1984

5. Which of the following policies of the Manchus was most effective in unifying southern Ming resistance to the new foreign dynasty?

(A) Chinese were forbidden from engaging in trade with the outside world.

(B) Chinese men were forced to wear their hair in a queue (ponytail).

(C) Chinese women were encouraged to marry Manchus.

(D) Confucian scholars were removed from government positions.

6. A historical analogy to the Manchu treatment of Han Chinese is

(A) Elizabeth I's sumptuary laws dictating styles of dress by social class

(B) medieval European laws that Jews wear distinctive hats and badges

(C) the Turkish policy in the early nineteenth century of replacing the turban with the fez hat

(D) detailed Spanish-American classifications of Native, African, and Spanish ancestry

1450 to 1750 C.E.

Questions 7–8 refer to the passage below.

"Those that arriv'd at these Islands from the remotest parts of Spain, and who pride themselves in the Name of Christians, steer'd Two courses principally, in order to the Extirpation, and Exterminating of this [Native] People from the face of the Earth. The first whereof was raising an unjust, sanguinolent, cruel War. The other, by putting them to death, who hitherto, thirsted after their Liberty. . . : For they being taken off in War, none but Women and Children were permitted to enjoy the benefit of that Country-Air, on whom they did in succeeding times lay such a heavy Yoak, that the very Brutes were more happy than they. . . .

Finally, in one word, their Ambition and Avarice, than which the heart of Man never entertained greater, and the vast Wealth of those Regions; the Humility and Patience of the Inhabitants (which made their approach to these Lands more facil and easie) did much promote the business: Whom they so despicably contemned, that they treated them (I speak of things which I was an Eye Witness of, without the least fallacy) not as Beasts, which I cordially wished they would, but as the most abject dung and filth of the Earth. . . ."

Excerpt from Bartolome de las Casas's *A Brief Account of the Destruction of the Indies*, 1552

7. The purpose of the *encomienda* system was to

    (A) eliminate the Native American population

    (B) prevent the Atlantic slave trade from increasing

    (C) supply Europeans with a steady supply of labor

    (D) give Native Americans economic opportunities

8. Which of the following best describes the historical effect of de las Casas's report?

    (A) It showed that the inhumanity of the colonial system was recognized at the time.

    (B) The King decreed that African slavery should replace the *encomienda* system.

    (C) Responsibility for Native employment was transferred to the Church.

    (D) Colonial elites decided to introduce a more humane labor system.

Questions 9–10 refer to the image below.

Leonardo da Vinci, *Vitruvian Man*, 1490 C.E.

9. The picture above and the three statements below refer to which of the following?

    - Works of Leonardo da Vinci
    - Importance of the Medici family
    - Wealth of Mediterranean Sea trade

    (A) Northern Renaissance

    (B) Protestant Reformation

    (C) Enlightenment

    (D) Italian Renaissance

10. Art and literature created during the Italian Renaissance

    (A) reflected a shift toward realism, scientific study, and humanist thought

    (B) successfully reinforced the widespread religious devotion and faith in the Catholic Church of the time

    (C) shows how women enjoyed more freedom than during the Middle Ages

    (D) drew sole influence from the current time, not from other cultures nor time periods

Part B: Key Topics

This key topics list is the same as the list in the Test What You Already Know section earlier in this chapter. Based on what you have now learned, ask yourself the following questions:

- Can I describe this key topic?
- Can I discuss this key topic in the context of other events?
- Could I correctly answer a multiple-choice question about this key topic?
- Could I correctly answer a free-response question about this key topic?

Check off the key topics if you can answer "yes" to at least three of these questions.

European Exploration

- ☐ Caravel
- ☐ Columbus
- ☐ Conquest of Constantinople
- ☐ Ottoman

Trading-Post Empires

- ☐ Joint-stock companies

Columbian Exchange

- ☐ Columbian Exchange

Mercantilism: The Role and Impact of Silver

- ☐ Mercantilism

The Role and Impact of Sugar

- ☐ Sugar cultivation

State-Building

- ☐ Creoles
- ☐ *Daimyos*
- ☐ *Encomienda*
- ☐ Gunpowder
- ☐ *Haciendas*
- ☐ Manchu
- ☐ *Mestizos*
- ☐ Mughal empire
- ☐ Mulattos
- ☐ Peter the Great
- ☐ Songhai
- ☐ Tokugawa shogunate
- ☐ Triangular trade

Cultural and Intellectual Changes

- ☐ Printing press
- ☐ Protestant Reformation
- ☐ Scientific Revolution

The Environment

- ☐ Little Ice Age

Tally Your Results for Part A and Part B

Part A: Check your answers and count the number of questions you got correct.

1.	D	6.	C
2.	B	7.	C
3.	D	8.	A
4.	D	9.	D
5.	B	10.	A

_____ out of 10 questions

Part B: Count the number of key topics you checked off.

_____ out of 25 key topics

Next Step: Compare your Test What You Already Know results to these Test What You Learned results to see how exam-ready you are for AP World History Period 4: 1450 to 1750 C.E.

CHAPTER 6

Period 5:
1750 to 1900 C.E.

LEARNING OBJECTIVES

After studying this time period, you will be able to:

- Describe the effects, both positive and negative, of legal systems and independence movements on race, class, and gender.

- Describe the interaction of specialized labor systems and social hierarchies.

- Demonstrate ways in which economic systems, and values and ideologies, have influenced each other.

- Explain how production and commerce develop and change.

- Explain how societies can be changed or challenged over time.

- Describe the impact of ideology and belief on populations.

- Assess the impact of technology and exchange networks on the environment.

CHAPTER OUTLINE

TIMELINE

Date	Region	Event
1756–1763	Americas & Europe	French and Indian War & Seven Years' War
1776	Americas	American Revolution
1789	Europe	French Revolution
1804	Americas	Haitian independence
1820	Americas	Independence in Latin America
1839	East Asia	First Opium War in China
1848	Europe	European Revolutions
1853	East Asia	Commodore Perry opens Japan
1857	South Asia	Sepoy Mutiny
1863	Americas	Emancipation Proclamation
1871	Europe	German unification
1898	Americas	Spanish-American War
1899–1902	Africa	Boer War

TEST WHAT YOU ALREADY KNOW

Part A: Quiz

Questions 1–3 refer to the map below.

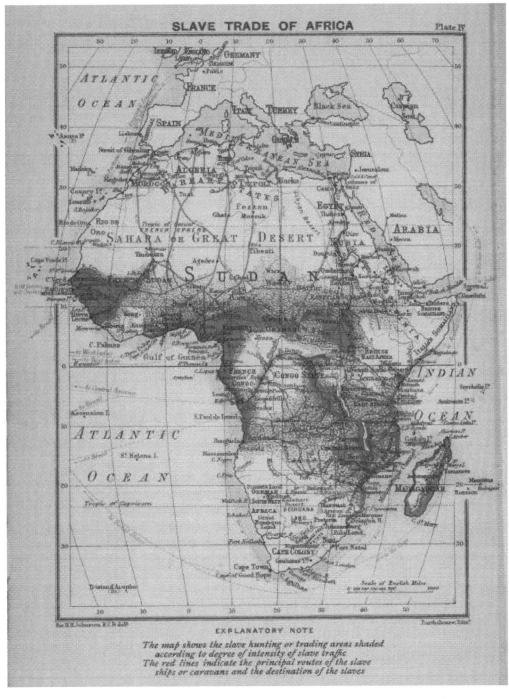

"Slave Trade of Africa," author Harry Hamilton Johnston and cartographer
John George Bartholomew, 1899

1. Based on the map, which of the following was a consequence of the transatlantic slave trade?

   (A) Christianity became the dominant religion in North Africa.

   (B) Trading routes in West Africa moved towards coastal regions.

   (C) The majority of African slaves were transported to India and other Asian regions.

   (D) Permanent European settlements, such as Cape Colony in South Africa, formed to support slave traders.

2. Which of the following developments of this period least supported the trade demonstrated on the map?

   (A) The diffusion of Islam through Africa

   (B) Improvements in maritime technology

   (C) The production of gunpowder in Europe

   (D) The establishment of colonies in the Americas

3. Which of the following most strongly contributed to the increase of the trade demonstrated on the map during the eighteenth century?

   (A) Industrialization

   (B) Sugar plantations

   (C) Absolute monarchies

   (D) Laissez-faire capitalism

Questions 4–6 refer to the following passage.

"Where the money is to come from which will defray this enormous annual expense of three millions sterling, and all those other debts, I know not; unless the author of *Common Sense*, or some other ingenious projector, can discover the Philosopher's Stone, by which iron and other base metals may be transmuted into gold. Certain I am that our commerce and agriculture, the two principal sources of our wealth, will not support such an expense. The whole of our exports from the Thirteen United Colonies, in the year 1769, amounted only to £2,887,898 sterling; which is not so much, by near half a million, as our annual expense would be were we independent of Great Britain."

Charles Inglis, Anglican clergyman of Trinity Church in New York City, New York, 1776

4. Based on this passage and your knowledge of world history, what were the primary motivations of proponents of the American Revolution, such as Thomas Paine?

   (A) Concerns that Great Britain would not allow the colonies to share the economic developments of the Industrial Revolution

   (B) Aspirations to expand industries such as metalwork in the colonies

   (C) Abstract ideals, as described by philosophers such as Montesquieu and Locke

   (D) Desires to attain freedom from the Anglican church and practice their faith with simplicity instead of ornamentation

5. In contrast to the American Revolution, the French Revolution

   (A) was caused by tensions in a colonial relationship with a distant imperial power

   (B) saw the wealthiest members of society be the main proponents of political change

   (C) was fueled by widespread discontent over feudal obligations to nobles and to the crown

   (D) based much of its revolutionary rhetoric on Enlightenment ideas and philosophies

6. Which of the following economic models contributed to the financial hardships described in the passage?

   (A) Mercantilism

   (B) Feudalism

   (C) Monarchism

   (D) Liberalism

Questions 7–10 refer to the following passage.

"I anticipate an excellent effect by and by from the impressions which the yet wilder envoys and Sirdars of Chitral and Yassin will carry with them from Delhi, and propagate throughout that important part of our frontier where the very existence of the British Government has hitherto been almost unrealised, except as that of a very weak power, popularly supposed in Kafirstan to be exceedingly afraid of Russia. Two Burmese noblemen, from the remotest part of Burmah, said to me: 'The King of Burmah fancies he is the greatest prince upon earth. When we go back, we shall tell all his people that he is nobody. Never since the world began has there been in it such a power as we have witnessed here.' These Burmese are writing a journal or memoir of their impressions and experiences at Delhi, of which they have promised me a copy. I have no doubt it will be very curious and amusing. Kashmir and some other native princes have expressed a wish to present your Majesty with an imperial crown of great value; but as each insists upon it that the crown shall be exclusively his own gift, I have discouraged an idea which, if carried out, would embarrass your Majesty with the gift of half a dozen different crowns, and probably provoke bitter heart-burnings amongst the donors. The Rajpootana Chiefs talk of erecting a marble statue of the Empress on the spot where the assemblage was held; and several native noblemen have already intimated to me their intention of building bridges, or other public works, and founding charities, to be called after your Majesty in commemoration of the event."

Excerpt from Lady Betty Balfour's *The History of Lord Lytton's Indian Administration*, 1899

7. The Indian National Congress and the Pan-African Congress were important examples of

   (A) economic alliances between countries in the developing world

   (B) nationalist organizations aimed at removing European control

   (C) international organizations with the goal of preventing Cold War conflicts

   (D) nongovernment organizations aimed at bringing industrialization to Asian and African countries

8. Toussaint L'Ouverture, Simón Bolívar, and Miguel Hidalgo y Costilla

   (A) supported the Reconquista

   (B) led independence movements

   (C) advocated against the abolishment of slavery

   (D) believed in communist-inspired revolutions

9. One result of the revolt in Saint-Domingue in the 1790s was that

   (A) the United States lost some of its Latin American territory

   (B) Haiti established an absolute monarchy

   (C) Saint-Domingue imported more slaves from West Africa

   (D) the largest West Indies colony abolished slavery

10. Which of the following statements correctly describes the Sepoy Mutiny of 1857?

   (A) It began after a rumor spread that British gunpowder cartridges contained pork and beef fat.

   (B) It had early beginnings during discussions in the Indian National Congress.

   (C) It was characterized by bitter warfare between Muslim and Hindu sepoys.

   (D) It resulted in 300 million Indians ruled under the British East India Company.

Part B: Key Topics

The following is a list of the major people, places, and events for Period 5: 1750 to 1900 C.E. You will very likely see many of these on the AP World History exam.

For each key topic, ask yourself the following questions:

- Can I describe this key topic?
- Can I discuss this key topic in the context of other events?
- Could I correctly answer a multiple-choice question about this key topic?
- Could I correctly answer a free-response question about this key topic?

Check off the key topics if you can answer "yes" to at least three of these questions.

Revolutions and Independence Movements

- ☐ American Revolution
- ☐ Enlightenment
- ☐ French Revolution
- ☐ Haitian Revolution
- ☐ Latin American independence movements
- ☐ Maroon

Nationalism and the Nation State

- ☐ Nationalism

Industrialization

- ☐ Adam Smith
- ☐ Factory system
- ☐ Global division of labor
- ☐ Imperialism
- ☐ Railroads
- ☐ Second Industrial Revolution

Reactions to Industrialization

- ☐ Communism
- ☐ Liberalism
- ☐ Socialism

Reform

- ☐ Boxer Rebellion
- ☐ First Opium War
- ☐ Meiji
- ☐ Second Opium War
- ☐ Self-Strengthening Movement
- ☐ Taiping Rebellion
- ☐ Tanzimât Movement

Imperialism and Its Impact

- ☐ Congo Free State
- ☐ Sepoy Mutiny of 1857
- ☐ Social Darwinism

Legacies of Imperialism

☐ Chinese Exclusion Act

☐ Indentured servants

Emancipation

☐ Emancipation of slaves

☐ Feminism

Tally Your Results for Part A and Part B

Part A: Check your answers and count the number of questions you got correct.

1.	B	6.	A
2.	A	7.	B
3.	B	8.	B
4.	C	9.	D
5.	C	10.	A

_____ out of 10 questions

Part B: Count the number of key topics you checked off.

_____ out of 30 key topics

Next Steps:

- Review the quiz explanations in the back of the book.
- Read the Rapid Review section.
- Complete the Test What You Learned section and review the quiz explanations.

RAPID REVIEW

Summary—Period 5: 1750 to 1900 C.E.

1. Industrialization led the world to become truly interdependent. Industrialized nations in search of raw materials and new markets often colonized areas to advance their economic interests.

2. Populations grew, and many people migrated to cities in search of work in factories. Free-wage laborers were more desirable than forced labor in this new market-driven economy. As a result, slaves and serfs were emancipated.

3. Women gained some economic opportunities in the factories but were paid considerably less than their male counterparts. These new economic opportunities and Enlightenment ideals pushed women to fight for political rights as well.

4. The working class emerged as a force for change. Through organization into unions, these workers were able to advocate for improving their dangerous and oppressive working conditions.

5. Western culture strongly influenced many Asian and African areas through colonization. At the same time, Asian and African culture and art strongly influenced European intellectuals and artists. Enlightenment ideals such as equality, freedom of speech, and freedom of religion became very influential in many parts of the world, yet in other parts, traditional organized religion maintained power and influence.

6. The ideas of the Enlightenment said that the government was responsible to its people, inspiring revolutions and independence movements and pushing some governments to experiment with democratic values. This democracy, however, proved to extend to a limited class of people. "The nation" and nationalism became the new concepts of identity in the nineteenth century and would soon spread to many parts of the world.

Key Topics—Period 5: 1750 to 1900 C.E.

Remember that the AP World History exam tests you on the depth of your knowledge, not just your ability to recall facts. While we have provided brief definitions here, you will need to know these terms in even more depth for the AP exam, including how terms connect to broader historical themes and understandings.

Revolutions and Independence Movements

- **American Revolution:** After American colonists served alongside the British in the French and Indian War, the Crown issued a series of taxes to recover the war debt. The colonists, angered that they were being taxed without representation, protested the taxes and began fighting for independence. Although the Revolutionary War itself lasted from 1775–1781, the signing of the Declaration of Independence in 1776 was significant in that it laid the foundations for the first large-scale democracy since Ancient Greece.

- **Enlightenment:** Post-Renaissance period in European history devoted to the study and exploration of new ideas in science, politics, the arts, and philosophy.

- **French Revolution:** Inspired by America's victory in its own revolution, the "commoners" of eighteenth-century France sought to create a new political and social order free from royal control. The Third Estate, who vastly outnumbered the First and Second Estates (clergy and nobility, respectively), created the National Assembly and issued the Declaration of the Rights of Man and of the Citizen. In response, the French faced war with the other European powers, in which they emerged victorious thanks to the leadership of Napoleon Bonaparte.

- **Haitian Revolution:** Led by Toussaint L'Ouverture, this slave revolt lasted from 1791–1804, after which the former French colony of Saint-Domingue became the independent nation of Haiti, the second independent nation in the Western Hemisphere and the world's first black republic.

- **Latin American independence movements:** Inspired by the success of the Haitian Revolution, these movements against Spanish colonial rule in Central and South America in the 1810s and 1820s led to the independence of every nation in those areas. Key leaders were Simón Bolívar, José de San Martín, and Bernardo O'Higgins.

- **Maroon:** Term for a nineteenth-century escaped slave in the Americas who settled in his or her own settlement away from plantations. They caused tensions with the colonial authorities. This term can also be used to describe their present-day descendants.

Nationalism and the Nation State

- **Nationalism:** As European empires began growing, the people in those empires began to see themselves as part of a group with common heritages, cultures, languages, and religions. This sense of national identity and pride fueled the expansion of empires and led to the unification of nations.

Industrialization

- **Adam Smith:** English economist whose 1776 work *The Wealth of Nations* advocated a laissez-faire policy toward economics (minimal government interference), making him one of the fathers of modern capitalism.

- **Factory system:** System of labor used in the Industrial Revolution. This involved rigorous mechanization and large numbers of unskilled workers to mass-produce goods that were once made skillfully by hand. In the nineteenth century, the use of interchangeable parts simplified assembly but made work repetitive.

- **Global division of labor:** With the Industrial Revolution underway, the European powers began devoting themselves to large-scale manufacturing and transportation, requiring raw materials like cotton from India, rubber from Brazil, and metals from Central Africa. As a result, industrialized societies grew at the expense of less industrial societies, providing an impetus for imperialist conquests later in the nineteenth century.

- **Imperialism:** As the nations of Europe began to industrialize in the nineteenth century, they needed sources of raw materials and markets for their goods. To prevent warfare among them, the European powers called the Berlin Conference in 1884 to divide the African continent into colonies and forge their new industrial empires. This has had significant effects, both positive and negative, on Africa ever since.

- **Railroads:** With the invention of the steam-powered locomotive in England in the 1820s, a "transportation revolution" began in which mass-produced goods could be transported overland more quickly and inexpensively than ever before. By 1900, virtually every industrialized nation had a well-developed railroad system.

- **Second Industrial Revolution:** In the late nineteenth century, revolutionary new methods of producing steel, chemicals, and electrical power changed society in Western Europe, Japan, and the United States by introducing new ways of working and living.

Reactions to Industrialization

- **Communism:** An extreme form of socialism in which governments make economic decisions for the people. Envisioned by Karl Marx and Friedrich Engels in 1848's *Communist Manifesto*, this system advocated the overthrow of the bourgeoisie (capitalists) by the proletariat (workers).

- **Liberalism:** As industry led to the growth of a middle class, philosophers and political scientists advocated systems of government based on constitutions, separation of powers, and natural rights. Based on the philosophies of the Enlightenment.

- **Socialism:** A utopian ideal in response to the poor conditions of factories and factory workers. In this radical form of society, the workers would run the economy in a self-sufficient manner and share everything equally, thereby overthrowing the moneyed classes.

Reform

- **Boxer Rebellion:** In response to the growth of Western economic privilege in China, a secret society of Chinese, backed by the anti-Western Empress Cixi, attacked Western soldiers and workers in 1900. A Western coalition defeated the Boxers and undermined the legitimacy of the Qing Dynasty.

- **First Opium War:** Instigated in 1839 after Chinese customs officials refused British imports of Indian opium (due to the addictive effects it had on Chinese workers), these wars weakened the Qing Dynasty and opened up China to commercial domination by the West for the next century.

1750 to 1900 C.E.

- **Meiji:** After witnessing the arrival of American commodore Matthew Perry in Edo Bay (Tokyo Bay) in 1854 by steamship, young reform-minded Japanese sought to overthrow the isolationist Tokugawa shogunate. They were successful and in 1868 installed Emperor Meiji, who led Japan through a period of rapid, Western-guided industrialization.

- **Second Opium War:** Lasting from 1856–1860, this war resulted from the Western European desire to further weaken Chinese sovereignty over trade, to legalize the opium trade, and to expand the export of indentured workers whose situations closely resembled slavery.

- **Self-Strengthening Movement:** An attempt by China, in the 1860s and 1870s, to modernize its military and economy under its own terms. Changes were minimal due to imperial resistance.

- **Taiping Rebellion:** In the 1850s and 1860s, Chinese scholar Hong Xiuquan led a Christian-based revolutionary movement to reform China's society. The violent reaction by the imperial court left China financially strained and caused the bloodiest civil war in world history.

- **Tanzimât Movement:** From 1839–1879, as the rest of the great empires were industrializing, the Ottoman Empire attempted this period of reform with a modernized infrastructure, a French legal code, and religious equality under the law.

Imperialism and Its Impact

- **Congo Free State:** Established in 1885 by Belgium's King Leopold II as his "Free State," in reality, this Central African colony was a series of large rubber plantations worked by forced labor. Brutal weather and working conditions made this one of the most heinous examples of imperialist power. In the 1960s, it declared independence and became Zaire; now, it goes by the name Democratic Republic of the Congo.

- **Sepoy Mutiny of 1857:** Fought in India between the British and the sepoys (Indian soldiers in British service) after rumors spread that the cartridges for their rifles were sealed in pork and beef tallow, thereby violating Hindu and Muslim religious taboos. The British victory strengthened the legitimacy of the Crown's rule, and the British went so far as to declare Queen Victoria "Empress of India."

- **Social Darwinism:** Popular nineteenth-century theory used to justify the rich getting richer and the poor getting poorer in industrial societies. It drew on evolutionary theorist Charles Darwin's view of "survival of the fittest."

Legacies of Imperialism

- **Chinese Exclusion Act:** Instituted in the United States in 1882, these acts severely limited Chinese immigration, which had been prevalent earlier in the century, as many Chinese came to California and other western states for the Gold Rush and to build the Transcontinental Railroad.

- **Indentured servants:** As the nations of the Americas and the European colonies began to emancipate African slaves, this system of labor became much more prevalent. Poorer laborers came to the Americas, where they lived and worked for a small wage in exchange for a promise of several years of work.

Emancipation

- **Emancipation of slaves:** With the emergence of a new liberal political spirit came the idea that slavery was incompatible with Enlightenment ideals of freedom. As industry made field work and slavery less profitable, wage labor became more profitable, since it made sense to reward harder workers with higher wages. From the 1830s to the 1880s, every industrialized nation and their colonies gradually abolished slavery.

- **Feminism:** As new economic systems emerged and more professional jobs emerged, women started pushing for political and economic rights, in a challenge to the Enlightenment's conservative views of women.

TEST WHAT YOU LEARNED

Part A: Quiz

Questions 1–3 refer to the following excerpt.

"When in the Course of human events it becomes necessary for one people to dissolve the political bands which have connected them with another and to assume among the Powers of the earth, the separate and equal station to which the Laws of Nature and of Nature's God entitle them, a decent respect to the opinions of mankind requires that they should declare the causes which impel them to the separation.

We hold these truths to be self-evident, that all men are created equal, that they are endowed by their Creator with certain unalienable Rights, that among these are Life, Liberty and the pursuit of Happiness. — That to secure these rights, Governments are instituted among Men, deriving their just powers from the consent of the governed, — That whenever any Form of Government becomes destructive of these ends, it is the Right of the People to alter or to abolish it, and to institute new Government, laying its foundation on such principles and organizing its powers in such form, as to them shall seem most likely to affect their Safety and Happiness. Prudence, indeed, will dictate that Governments long established should not be changed for light and transient causes; and accordingly, all experience hath shewn that mankind are more disposed to suffer, while evils are sufferable than to right themselves by abolishing the forms to which they are accustomed. But when a long train of abuses and usurpations, pursuing invariably the same Object evinces a design to reduce them under absolute Despotism, it is their right, it is their duty, to throw off such Government, and to provide new Guards for their future security. — Such has been the patient sufferance of these Colonies; and such is now the necessity which constrains them to alter their former Systems of Government. The history of the present King of Great Britain is a history of repeated injuries and usurpations, all having in direct object the establishment of an absolute Tyranny over these States. To prove this, let Facts be submitted to a candid world."

United States of America's Declaration of Independence, 1776

1. John Locke argued that

    (A) the Church should play a role in governmental affairs

    (B) humans are born with innate knowledge of moral truths

    (C) people have the right to revolt when the government violates their natural rights

    (D) the government should own the means of production

2. The American colonists successfully won their independence from Great Britain for all of the following reasons <u>except</u> that

    (A) the French decided to support the colonists against the British and provided military support

    (B) the geographic vastness of the colonies was a hindrance to the British effort

    (C) the use of conventional military tactics by Americans proved superior to British military strategies

    (D) Americans were more motivated because they were fighting for a cause they believed in

3. Which of the following correctly describes a consequence of the Seven Years' War?

    (A) Britain raised and imposed new taxes on the American colonies, angering colonists.

    (B) France gained significant North American territory, including what became known as Quebec.

    (C) The English government became less able to enforce laws within the American colonies.

    (D) Native American tribes experienced new peaceful, friendly relations with Anglo-American fur traders.

Questions 4–6 refer to the following image.

4. Built in 1883 in Tokyo, this building is an example of

   (A) Westernization in Japan during the Meiji era

   (B) architecture constructed in Japanese cities controlled by European trading companies

   (C) palace buildings designed for Tokugawa shoguns

   (D) Shōwa-era department store architecture

5. All of the following occurred during the Meiji Restoration <u>except</u>

   (A) the overthrow of the shogun and consolidation of power under the emperor

   (B) modern technology was created entirely independently

   (C) the feudal system of labor and land ownership was eliminated

   (D) a powerful army and navy were created

6. Japan was opened to trade with the West primarily as a result of which of the following?

   (A) Commodore Matthew Perry's diplomacy

   (B) Japan's desire to avoid being colonized

   (C) Demand for Western goods and technology

   (D) The leadership of the shogun

1750 to 1900 C.E.

Questions 7–10 refer to the following passage.

"You, O King, live beyond the confines of many seas, nevertheless, impelled by your humble desire to partake of the benefits of our civilisation, you have dispatched a mission respectfully bearing your memorial [message of goodwill]. Your envoy has crossed the seas and paid his respects at my court on the anniversary of my birthday. To show your devotion, you have also sent offerings of your country's produce.

I have perused your memorial. The earnest terms in which it is couched reveal a respectful humility on your part, which is highly praiseworthy. In consideration of the fact that your ambassador and his deputy have come a long way with your memorial and tribute, I have shown them high favour and have allowed them to be introduced into my presence. To manifest my indulgence, I have entertained them at a banquet and made them numerous gifts. I have also caused presents to be forwarded to the naval commander and 600 of his officers and men, although they did not come to Peking, so that they too may share in my all-embracing kindness.

As to your entreaty to send one of your nationals to be accredited to my Celestial Court, and to be in control of your country's trade with China, this request is contrary to all usage of my dynasty. It cannot possibly be entertained. It is true that Europeans, in the service of the dynasty, have been permitted to live at Peking—but they are compelled to adopt Chinese dress, they are strictly confined to their own precincts and are never permitted to return home. You are presumably familiar with our dynastic regulations.

It behoves you, O King, to respect my sentiments and to display even greater devotion and loyalty in future, so that, by perpetual submission to our Throne, you may secure peace and prosperity for your country hereafter."

Letter from Qing Emperor to King George III of England, 1793

7. The Opium Wars of the nineteenth century resulted in
   (A) the outbreak of the Taiping Rebellion
   (B) the restoration of the emperor, the downfall of the shogunate, and an industrialization program
   (C) China adopting the French legal code and, eventually, a group of young reformers installing a "puppet" emperor
   (D) China's sovereignty being weakened in order to facilitate free trade with both European empires and the United States

8. In the letter above, the Qing emperor
   (A) welcomed foreign investment
   (B) reaffirmed British trading rights
   (C) declined an offer to increase trade
   (D) declared his submission to George III

9. Which term fits best with the Chinese policy pursued at the time the letter to George III was written?
   (A) Laissez-faire
   (B) Isolationism
   (C) Communism
   (D) Democracy

10. The Revolution of 1911 that overthrew the Qing dynasty is most comparable to which of the following events?
    (A) The French Revolution
    (B) The Paris Commune
    (C) The American Revolution
    (D) The Young Turk Revolution

Part B: Key Topics

This key topics list is the same as the list in the Test What You Already Know section earlier in this chapter. Based on what you have now learned, ask yourself the following questions:

- Can I describe this key topic?
- Can I discuss this key topic in the context of other events?
- Could I correctly answer a multiple-choice question about this key topic?
- Could I correctly answer a free-response question about this key topic?

Check off the key topics if you can answer "yes" to at least three of these questions.

Revolutions and Independence Movements

- [ ] American Revolution
- [ ] Enlightenment
- [ ] French Revolution
- [ ] Haitian Revolution
- [ ] Latin American independence movements
- [ ] Maroon

Nationalism and the Nation State

- [ ] Nationalism

Industrialization

- [ ] Adam Smith
- [ ] Factory system
- [ ] Global division of labor
- [ ] Imperialism
- [ ] Railroads
- [ ] Second Industrial Revolution

Reactions to Industrialization

- [ ] Communism
- [ ] Liberalism
- [ ] Socialism

Reform

- [ ] Boxer Rebellion
- [ ] First Opium War
- [ ] Meiji
- [ ] Second Opium War
- [ ] Self-Strengthening Movement
- [ ] Taiping Rebellion
- [ ] Tanzimât Movement

Imperialism and Its Impact

- [ ] Congo Free State
- [ ] Sepoy Mutiny of 1857
- [ ] Social Darwinism

Legacies of Imperialism

☐ Chinese Exclusion Act

☐ Indentured servants

Emancipation

☐ Emancipation of slaves

☐ Feminism

Tally Your Results for Part A and Part B

Part A: Check your answers and count the number of questions you got correct.

1. C

2. C

3. A

4. A

5. B

6. B

7. D

8. C

9. B

10. A

_____ out of 10 questions

Part B: Count the number of key topics you checked off.

_____ out of 30 key topics

Next Step: Compare your Test What You Already Know results to these Test What You Learned results to see how exam-ready you are for AP World History Period 5: 1750 to 1900 C.E.

CHAPTER 7

Period 6: 1900 C.E. to the Present

LEARNING OBJECTIVES

After studying this time period, you will be able to:

- Analyze the influence of politics on states.

- Describe how societies rise and change because of race, class, and gender.

- Describe the impact of ideologies and beliefs on social hierarchies.

- Explain changes in social structures over time.

- Describe the role of the arts in both changing and reflecting society.

CHAPTER OUTLINE

TIMELINE

Date	Region	Event
1904–1905	Europe & East Asia	Russo-Japanese War
1908–1918	Mid East	Young Turk Era
1910–1920	Americas	Mexican Revolution
1911–1912	East Asia	Chinese Revolution
1914–1918	Europe	World War I
1917	Europe	Bolshevik Revolution
1918–1920	Europe	Russian Civil War
1919	Europe	Treaty of Versailles
1921–1928	Europe	Lenin's New Economic Policy
1923	Mid East	Republic of Turkey is established; end of the Ottoman Empire
1928–1932	Europe	First of Stalin's Five-Year Plans
1929	Americas	Great Depression begins
1931	East Asia	Japanese invade Manchuria
1933	Europe	Hitler's rise to power
1935	South Asia	Government of India Act
1937	East Asia	Japanese invasion of China
1939	Europe	German invasion of Poland
1945	Europe	End of World War II
1947	South Asia	Partition of India
1948	Europe	Marshall Plan
1948	Mid East	Creation of Israel
1948	Africa	Apartheid established in South Africa
1949	Europe	Division of Germany
1949	East Asia	People's Republic of China established
1950–1953	East Asia	Korean War
1958–1961	East Asia	China's Great Leap Forward
1959	Americas	Cuban Revolution
1962	Americas	Cuban Missile Crisis
1973	Mid East	Arab-Israeli War
1975	East Asia	Fall of Vietnam
1979	Mid East	Iranian Revolution
1980–1988	Mid East	Iran-Iraq War
1989	Europe	Fall of Berlin Wall
1990–1991	Mid East	Gulf War
1991	Europe	Fall of Soviet Union; end of the Cold War
2003	Mid East	Iraq War
2008–2010	Global	Economic crisis

1900 C.E. to Present

TEST WHAT YOU ALREADY KNOW

Part A: Quiz

Questions 1–2 refer to the passage below.

"The fanatical sermon delivered by Gapon, who had entirely forgotten his priestly dignity, and the criminal propaganda of his assistants belonging to the local revolutionary groups, excited the working population to such an extent that on January 9th enormous masses of people began to direct their course from all the suburbs of the city toward its center. And at the time that Gapon, continuing to influence the religious sentiment and loyalty of the people to their sovereign, previous to the beginning of the procession held religious service in the chapel of the Putilov Works for the welfare of their Majesties and distributed to the leaders icons, holy banners, and portraits of the sovereigns so as to give the demonstration the character of a religious procession, at the other end of the city a small group of workmen, led by true revolutionists, was erecting a barricade of telegraph-posts and wire and hoisted a red flag over it. Such a spectacle was so foreign to the general sentiment of the workmen that from the enormous crowd going toward the center of the city were heard the words: 'These are not our people, this does not concern us. These are students who are rioting.'

Notwithstanding this the crowds, electrified by the agitation, did not give way to the general police measures and even at the attacks of the cavalry. Excited by the opposition they met with, they began to attack the military forces, endeavoring to break through to the Winter Palace square, so that it was found necessary for the purpose of dispersing the crowds to use firearms, avoiding, as far as possible, making useless victims. This latter measure explains the comparatively small losses experienced by the enormous mass of people marching to the Winter Palace square. The military forces were obliged to shoot on the Schlusselburg Road, at the Narva Gate, near the Tritzky Bridge, on Fourth Street and the Little Perspective of the St. Basil Island, near the Alexander Garden, at the corner of the Nevsky Perspective and the Gogol Street, near the Police Bridge and on the Kasan Square."

Excerpt from Arthur Cassini's "Revolution in Russia: Bloody Sunday and the Constitution," 1914

1. The protesters described in this passage likely contributed to which of the following social movements?

   (A) Tanzimât

   (B) Socialism

   (C) Anti-nationalism

   (D) Self-Strengthening

2. Which of the following was a long-term consequence of the events depicted in the passage?

   (A) The Duma was permanently established.

   (B) Tsarist rule was ended.

   (C) Socialism was largely replaced by nationalism among the working class.

   (D) Russian revolutionary efforts further developed.

Questions 3–4 refer to the image below.

A Chinese elementary-school textbook shows a group of Red Guards, 1971

3. The image above best demonstrates Chinese efforts to

(A) counter anti-communist propaganda in Taiwan

(B) eliminate distinctions between rural and urban youth

(C) imitate Lenin's vision for the education of Soviet youth

(D) promote gender equality resulting from the Chinese Cultural Revolution

4. Which of the following best describes the impact of the Cultural Revolution?

(A) Literature, historical monuments, and cultural and religious sites were destroyed.

(B) China was transformed from an agrarian to an industrial economy.

(C) It created a climate more tolerant to diverse political ideology.

(D) It resulted in a return to traditional values, culture, and customs.

Questions 5–7 refer to the passage below.

"The Purposes of the United Nations are:

1. To maintain international peace and security, and to that end: to take effective collective measures for the prevention and removal of threats to the peace, and for the suppression of acts of aggression or other breaches of the peace, and to bring about by peaceful means, and in conformity with the principles of justice and international law, adjustment or settlement of international disputes or situations which might lead to a breach of the peace;

2. To develop friendly relations among nations based on respect for the principle of equal rights and self-determination of peoples, and to take other appropriate measures to strengthen universal peace;

3. To achieve international co-operation in solving international problems of an economic, social, cultural, or humanitarian character, and in promoting and encouraging respect for human rights and for fundamental freedoms for all without distinction as to race, sex, language, or religion; and

4. To be a centre for harmonizing the actions of nations in the attainment of these common ends."

Charter of the United Nations, 1945

5. Which of the following conflicts motivated the international community to form the United Nations?

(A) The Korean War

(B) The Cold War

(C) World War I

(D) World War II

6. Which of the following was a primary reason for the failure of the League of Nations?

(A) The refusal of the United States and Soviet Union to join as members

(B) Global economic fallout from the Great Depression

(C) Multiple conflicts which overtaxed the League's joint military forces

(D) The rising global threat of communism

7. The United Nations is committed to all of the following except

(A) personal freedoms

(B) diplomacy

(C) international trade

(D) self-governance

Questions 8–10 refer to the passage below.

"Over the following years much of Latin America saw an upsurge of rural guerrilla conflict and urban terrorism, in response to the persistence of stark social inequality and political repression. But this upsurge drew additional inspiration from the Cuban example, and in many cases Cuba provided training and material support to guerrillas."

"History of Latin America," *Encyclopaedia Britannica*

8. Over the last four decades of the twentieth century, the political structure of most Latin American countries changed

    (A) from democracy to communism

    (B) from communism to military dictatorship

    (C) from European colonial rule to independence

    (D) from dictatorship to democracy

9. The Sandinista National Liberation Front successfully overthrew Anastasio Somoza DeBayle in which country?

    (A) Cuba

    (B) Honduras

    (C) Nicaragua

    (D) Guatemala

10. While Cuba provided support to various guerrilla rebellions in Latin America after the Cuban Revolution, which country provided the most economic and military support to Cuba?

    (A) Soviet Union

    (B) Brazil

    (C) United States

    (D) Spain

Part B: Key Topics

The following is a list of the major people, places, and events for Period 6: 1900 C.E. to the Present. You will very likely see many of these on the AP World History exam.

For each key topic, ask yourself the following questions:

- Can I describe this key topic?
- Can I discuss this key topic in the context of other events?
- Could I correctly answer a multiple-choice question about this key topic?
- Could I correctly answer a free-response question about this key topic?

Check off the key topics if you can answer "yes" to at least three of these questions.

World War I

- ☐ League of Nations
- ☐ Mohandas Gandhi
- ☐ Total war
- ☐ World War I

Global Depression

- ☐ Great Depression
- ☐ World War II

Rise of Fascist and Totalitarian States

- ☐ Adolf Hitler
- ☐ Benito Mussolini
- ☐ Fascism
- ☐ Joseph Stalin

World War II

- ☐ Cold War
- ☐ Firebombing
- ☐ Nuclear bomb
- ☐ United Nations

The Cold War

- ☐ European Union
- ☐ Non-Aligned Movement
- ☐ Proxy wars
- ☐ Vietnam
- ☐ Warsaw Pact

Revolutions

- ☐ Fidel Castro
- ☐ Great Leap Forward
- ☐ Mao Zedong
- ☐ Vladimir Lenin

Independence and Nationalist Movements

- ☐ Algeria
- ☐ Ho Chi Minh
- ☐ Indian National Congress
- ☐ Indian/Pakistan partition
- ☐ Muhammad Ali Jinnah

Political Reform and Economic Changes

- ☐ Deng Xiaoping
- ☐ NATO
- ☐ Tiananmen Square

Technology, Populations, and the Environment

- ☐ Cholera
- ☐ Green Revolution
- ☐ HIV/AIDS

Social and Cultural Changes

- ☐ Liberation theology in Latin America
- ☐ Pan-Africanism

Tally Your Results for Part A and Part B

Part A: Check your answers and count the number of questions you got correct.

1.	B	6.	A
2.	D	7.	C
3.	D	8.	D
4.	A	9.	C
5.	D	10.	A

_____ out of 10 questions

Part B: Count the number of key topics you checked off.

_____ out of 36 key topics

Next Steps:

- Review the quiz explanations in the back of the book.
- Read the Rapid Review section.
- Complete the Test What You Learned section and review the quiz explanations.

RAPID REVIEW

Summary—Period 6: 1900 C.E. to the Present

1. Due to improvements in health care and the decrease of the death rate, the world population went from 1 billion people in 1900 to over 6 billion. The movement of people has also increased throughout the world, with many in search of better economic opportunities. Some refugees, too, are being forced to leave their homelands.

2. Traditional social structures have been challenged as a result of movements that have attempted to empower the working class, such as the introduction of communist governments in various parts of the world.

3. Women gained the right to vote in many parts of the world, as well as access to new economic opportunities and education. The development of the birth control pill empowered women by allowing them to control their own reproductive systems.

4. The world became more and more integrated through technology, cultures have blended, and some came to dominate. At the same time, religious fundamentalism has developed in some regions, possibly to combat Western-dominated global culture.

5. The rise in the nation-state and nationalism has led to the adoption of political systems from totalitarianism to democracy. At the same time, the rise of a more globally connected world may blur the lines of the nation-state.

6. The world wars demonstrated the influence of technology on warfare, but also indicated the decline of Europe as the dominant global power. Colonial areas asserted themselves and fought for independence, but were later faced with a new global conflict called the Cold War. Since the end of the Cold War, nations have made attempts at both economic and political reforms, and international and multinational organizations have made attempts to establish a new world order.

Key Topics—Period 6: 1900 C.E. to the Present

Remember that the AP World History exam tests you on the depth of your knowledge, not just your ability to recall facts. While we have provided brief definitions here, you will need to know these terms in even more depth for the AP exam, including how terms connect to broader historical themes and understandings.

1900 C.E. to Present

World War I

- **League of Nations:** As part of U.S. President Woodrow Wilson's plans for postwar peace (the Fourteen Points), a multinational coalition was created to prevent further war through open negotiations. Ironically, the United States never became a member. The power of the League was delegitimized in the 1930s with the Japanese invasion of Manchuria, the Spanish Civil War, and the Italian invasion of Ethiopia.

- **Mohandas Gandhi:** Regarded as the most influential leader of the Indian Independence movement, the Mahatma ("Great Soul") was known for his grassroots approach to protest. Using a combination of religious ideals, Gandhi and his followers used civil disobedience and nonviolence to help India gain its independence. Although Gandhi was murdered just five months after independence, his legacy influenced such leaders as Dr. Martin Luther King and the Dalai Lama.

- **Total war:** Warfare in which the entire nation devotes its efforts to large-scale war, usually with the aim to completely eliminate an enemy threat. The two world wars are well-known examples.

- **World War I:** Initially known as the Great War, this total war officially began in 1914 with the assassination of Austrian Archduke Franz Ferdinand, but it was rooted in secret alliances, nationalism, and militarism among the European powers. Its end in 1918 left Europe with many unresolved issues that would be settled in World War II.

Global Depression

- **Great Depression:** Generally considered to have happened from 1929–1939, this global economic recession was caused by a variety of factors, including Europe's relative inability to recover economically from World War I and the collapse of the American stock market in the wake of increased investment. Politically, this caused many around the world to favor government intervention in the economy.

- **World War II:** Officially taking place from 1939–1945 (though some historians argue it started as far back as 1931), this total war pitted the Axis powers (Germany, Italy, and Japan) against the Allied powers (Britain, France, the Soviet Union, and the United States) in a truly global war that attempted to resolve post-World War I issues. The outcome of this war changed the world's political and economic history.

Rise of Fascist and Totalitarian States

- **Adolf Hitler:** Austrian-born leader who, after witnessing Germany's humiliating defeat in World War I, vowed to restore Germany to its former glory through militarism, ultranationalism, extreme violence, and anti-Semitism. Using propaganda and indoctrination, Hitler led the Nazi Party and became chancellor of Germany in 1933.

- **Benito Mussolini:** Leader of Italy's "Blackshirts" and key proponent of fascism as an anti-communist movement. In 1922, he and his followers successfully deposed King Vittorio Emmanuel II and established Italy as a military dictatorship.

- **Fascism:** In response to the rise of communism in Eastern Europe after World War I, this political and economic system emerged in Italy in the 1920s under the leadership of Benito Mussolini. Key ideas of fascism include extreme nationalism, militarism, dictatorship, and the "corporate state," in which governments ally with big businesses to build themselves up economically.

- **Joseph Stalin:** Successor to V. I. Lenin, this dictator solidified his rule and used an extreme form of communism (Stalinism) to rule the U.S.S.R. from 1927 to his death in 1953. His political ideology included centralized planning of the economy, collective farms, and purging of all dissent.

World War II

- **Cold War:** Ideological struggle pitting the United States and the Soviet Union against each other for global political hegemony, 1949–1993.

- **Firebombing:** Use of incendiary bombs during warfare, particularly from airplanes. The bombs, filled with either thermite or napalm, cause massive burning of large areas at any given time and were particularly used in World War II and the Vietnam War.

- **Nuclear bomb:** Developed in the United States in the 1940s, this weapon ended World War II when it was dropped on the Japanese cities of Hiroshima and Nagasaki. Although it killed over 150,000 people, historians argue that it saved lives by forcing Japan's immediate surrender. Although the following decades were marked by a race for nuclear supremacy, it should be noted that the bombings of Hiroshima and Nagasaki were the only times that nuclear bombs were used in warfare.

- **United Nations:** Founded in 1945 with the intent of settling postwar concerns and recovering war-torn nations, this international organization is responsible for peacekeeping tasks around the world, with the cooperation of its member nations.

The Cold War

- **European Union:** First formed in 1993, a continent-wide alliance of economic regulation that now has over 25 members, including several formerly communist countries. Originally formed as the European Economic Community by six European nations in 1957 as an economic alliance designed to eliminate trade barriers, end reliance on the United States, and ease tensions between former rivals.

- **Non-Aligned Movement:** In the wake of the Cold War, the nations of Africa, Asia, and Latin America were ushered into alliances with the United States and the Soviet Union. Some nations chose not to ally. The first formal conference took place in 1955 and was led by Nehru of India and Nasser of Egypt. By the end of the Cold War, over 100 nations had announced that they would remain neutral in the context of the Cold War.

- **Proxy wars:** Particularly common during the Cold War, these are wars that are instigated or supported by a major power, but not fought by them. Instead, these are fought by proxy, or by another power in an attempt to help the major power achieve its aims.

- **Vietnam:** Nation in Southeast Asia that, in the wake of France's defeat at Dien Bien Phu in 1954, was divided into two. The rise of Ho Chi Minh, a Marxist leader of nationalist forces, led to one of the longest, bloodiest military engagements of the Cold War: the Vietnam War. Ho's victory caused Vietnam to turn communist.

- **Warsaw Pact:** Formed in 1955 by the Soviet Union and seven Eastern Bloc countries, this defensive alliance sought to counteract the growing influence of NATO.

Revolutions

- **Fidel Castro:** Guerrilla leader of Cuba who, in 1959, deposed the dictatorship of Fulgencio Batista in an attempt to resolve income inequities. By 1961, he had made Cuba into a Soviet ally and caused great tensions between Cuba and its nearby neighbor, the United States. He led Cuba until he resigned in 2008, citing health concerns and handing over rule to his brother Raul.

- **Great Leap Forward:** Mao Zedong's ambitious plan, starting in 1958, to collectivize all aspects of the economy, most notably by having communal houses with backyard furnaces for steel production. After just five years and the deaths of millions of Chinese from starvation, the program was declared a failure, and Mao laid the groundwork for his Cultural Revolution in the 1960s.

- **Mao Zedong:** Leader of the Chinese Communist Party in the 1920s and 1930s, he reemerged in the 1940s as he and his followers fought the Nationalists (Kuomintang). In 1949, Mao declared victory and made himself leader of the People's Republic of China, a position he held until his death in 1976. He was also known for radical national initiatives like the Great Leap Forward and the Cultural Revolution.

- **Vladimir Lenin:** Leader of the Bolsheviks in Russia during World War I, a society of radical communists whose aim was to overthrow the tsar. With his return to Russia in 1917 and the Russian Civil War in the years following, Lenin and his Bolsheviks seized power and transformed Russia into the Communist Union of Soviet Socialist Republics.

Independence and Nationalist Movements

- **Algeria:** Largest nation in Northwest Africa, this former French colony gained its independence in 1962 after a long war, in which nationalist troops fought against French leaders and their broken promises of better lives and freedom during the Anglo-American occupation of North Africa.

- **Ho Chi Minh:** Vietnamese nationalist leader who fought against the Japanese during the Axis occupation of French Vietnam in World War II and then fought against the French after the war. When the Soviets and communist Chinese offered support to him and North Vietnam during the Vietnam War, the Americans responded by supporting anti-communist South Vietnam. The resulting war led to Ho's leadership of North Vietnam.

- **Indian National Congress:** Founded in 1885 by British-educated Hindu leaders, this political party gained traction in 1919 when the failure of the Rowlatt Acts gave them more power. In the decades that followed, they became the political wing of the movement for Indian Independence and to this day still play an influential role in India's government.

- **Indian/Pakistan Partition:** In 1947, the nations of India and Pakistan both became independent from Great Britain. India was dominated by the Hindus, and Pakistan, divided into West and East Pakistan (modern-day Bangladesh), was Muslim dominated. Tensions between Hindus and Muslims in South Asia continue to this day, as evidenced by the continued conflict over the disputed region of Kashmir.

- **Muhammad Ali Jinnah:** Prior to 1920, this political leader had favored an alliance of Hindus and Muslims in the creation of one unified, independent India. However, in response to the popular rise of Mahatma Gandhi, Jinnah became leader of the Muslim League, a party devoted to the creation of a Muslim-led state in South Asia to prevent domination by the Hindu majority. In 1947, he became the first leader of his new nation, Pakistan, and led it for the last year of his life.

Political Reform and Economic Changes

- **Deng Xiaoping:** Premier of communist China from Mao Zedong's death in 1976 to his own death in 1997, he instituted the Four Modernizations in an attempt to introduce capitalist reform in China. His non-democratic policies, though, drew the ire of educated Chinese, culminating in the Tiananmen Square uprising of 1989.

- **NATO:** North Atlantic Treaty Organization. Founded in 1949 by the nations of North America and Europe, this defensive alliance sought to contain the spread of communism in Eastern Europe.

- **Tiananmen Square:** Large public square in Beijing, China. Site of a 1989 conflict between students, protesting for democratic reform, and the Chinese military, defending the leadership of Deng Xiaoping.

Technology, Populations, and the Environment

- **Cholera:** Acute bacterial infection of the small intestine that was pandemic in the nineteenth century. Generally speaking, it affects people in developing nations more, since it spreads easily through contaminated drinking water.

- **Green Revolution:** Beginning in the 1960s, this movement introduced new technologies and high-yield seed strains in an attempt to boost food production in developing countries. Initially successful in Mexico and India, its terminology has been called into question due to the increased use of chemical fertilizers that pollute the environment.

- **HIV/AIDS:** Human Immunodeficiency Virus and Acquired Immunodeficiency Syndrome. The virus attacks the human body's immune system, leaving patients susceptible to lethal diseases that slowly kill them. First reported in the United States in 1981, its unknown origins and rapid spread have made it one of the most recent epidemics and a symbol of the interconnected nature of today's world.

Social and Cultural Changes

- **Liberation theology in Latin America:** A movement led by the Catholic Church beginning in the 1950s, this new religious movement emphasizes that the teachings of Christ can help liberate people from the political and economic injustices of poverty.

- **Pan-Africanism:** The idea that people of the African continent have a shared heritage and should unify in that regard, despite the fact that they live in different nations. This attitude was the basis of many African independence movements after World War II.

TEST WHAT YOU LEARNED

Part A: Quiz

Questions 1–2 refer to the map below.

THE VOYAGES OF HMS ORVIETO 1915–1918

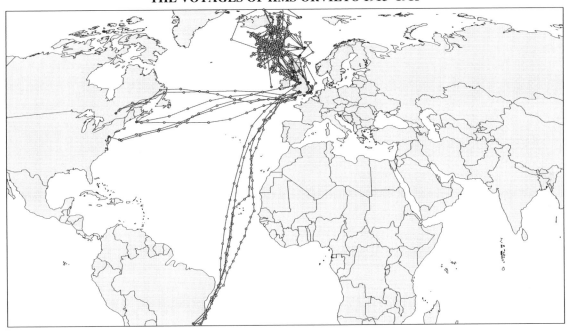

1. The travels of the *H.M.S. Orvieto* best illustrate

    (A) the success of the German U-boat
        campaign

    (B) the role of Atlantic trade in the Allied
        victory during World War I

    (C) the vast reach of British imperial territory

    (D) the superiority of newly invented ironclad
        ships

2. A major impact of World War I in Latin
    America was

    (A) a population explosion as Americans
        migrated to Latin America to avoid the
        draft

    (B) a population decline as many people
        volunteered to fight in the conflict,
        prompted by ideological sympathy

    (C) a temporary economic boom because of
        demand for wartime products such as
        Chilean nitrate

    (D) a temporary economic decline because of
        low international demand for luxury goods
        during World War I

Questions 3–4 refer to the image below.

CONTRACTION OF WORLD TRADE, 1929–1933

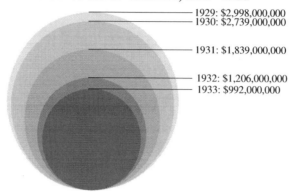

1929: $2,998,000,000
1930: $2,739,000,000

1931: $1,839,000,000

1932: $1,206,000,000
1933: $992,000,000

SOURCE: Charles P. Kindleberger, *The World in Depression* 1929–1933

3. Which of the following was a major impact of the Great Depression on colonial territories?

   (A) Many territories were granted independence because the governments of industrialized capitalist countries could no longer support them.

   (B) Demand for raw materials continued during the Great Depression while demand for finished goods dropped.

   (C) Local economies were devastated because many colonies relied on exports like rubber and cocoa, which were vulnerable to fluctuations in the world market.

   (D) Economic and social tensions caused many colonies to revolt and establish independent communist governments.

4. All of the following are true regarding the global economy during the Great Depression <u>except</u>

   (A) economic hardship led to social instability and political extremism

   (B) countries responded by lowering tariffs and encouraging imports

   (C) global unemployment rose to double digits

   (D) U.S. bank failures led to a collapse of world financial centers

Questions 5–6 refer to the passage below.

"Study the Soviet Union's merits and support all the Soviet Union's correct positions. There are two good things about the reactionaries' anti-Chinese [activities]: one is that they have revealed the reactionaries, reducing their prestige among the people; the second is that they have stimulated the consciousness of the majority of the peoples in the world, who can then see that reactionary imperialism, nationalism, and revisionism are enemies, swindlers, and contraband, whereas the Chinese flag is bright red.

The whole world is very bright. The darker the clouds, the greater the light.

Marxism and Leninism will get the greatest development in China. There is no doubt of this.

Khrushchev and his group are very naïve. He does not understand Marxism-Leninism and is easily fooled by imperialism.

He does not understand China, to an extreme extent. He doesn't research [China] and believes a whole bunch of incorrect information. He gives irresponsible talks. If he doesn't correct [his mistakes], in a few years he'll be completely bankrupt (after 8 years).

He panics over China. The panic has reached its extreme.

He has two main fears: imperialism and Chinese Communism.

He fears that Eastern European or other Communist parties will believe us and not them. His world view is pragmatism. This is an extreme kind of subjective idealism. He lacks a workable agenda and will follow gain wherever it goes.

The Soviet people are good as is the [Soviet] party. There is something not good about the style of the party and people, a somewhat metaphysical style, a kind of capitalist-liberalism inherited from history. Lenin died early and didn't have time to reform it."

Mao Zedong, "An Outline for a Speech on the International Situation," 1959

5. Which of the following was true of the Russian communist revolution, but was <u>not</u> true of China's communist revolution?

    (A) The government instituted a Five-Year Plan.

    (B) The government struggled to apply Marxist ideals to a largely agricultural economy.

    (C) The government derived support for communism mainly from the cities.

    (D) The government used totalitarian methods to eliminate opposition.

6. Which of the following best describes a cause for the Sino-Soviet split?

    (A) Diverging ideology and national interests

    (B) Competition over colonial territory

    (C) Personality clashes between Soviet and Chinese leadership

    (D) Détente between the United States and the Soviet Union

Questions 7–8 refer to the passage below.

"Are these the beginnings of profound changes in the Soviet state? Or are they token gestures, intended to raise false hopes in the West, or to strengthen the Soviet system without changing it? We welcome change and openness; for we believe that freedom and security go together, that the advance of human liberty can only strengthen the cause of world peace. There is one sign the Soviets can make that would be unmistakable, that would advance dramatically the cause of freedom and peace.

General Secretary Gorbachev, if you seek peace, if you seek prosperity for the Soviet Union and Eastern Europe, if you seek liberalization: Come here to this gate! Mr. Gorbachev, open this gate! Mr. Gorbachev, tear down this wall!"

Ronald Reagan, "Tear Down This Wall," 1987

7. Which of the following regimes is most associated with policies of "openness" and "restructuring"?

   (A) The People's Republic of China under Mao Zedong

   (B) The Soviet Union under Gorbachev

   (C) The Soviet Union under Stalin

   (D) Cuba under Fidel Castro

8. Which of the following did <u>not</u> lead to the collapse of the Soviet Union?

   (A) The reunification of Germany

   (B) The Soviet invasion of Afghanistan

   (C) The Polish Solidarity movement

   (D) The implementation of *glasnost* and *perestroika*

Questions 9–10 refer to the passage below.

"One of the last countries to return to democracy was Chile, where the Pinochet dictatorship had been more successful than most. . . . After first imposing harsh readjustments and committing its share of mistakes, it had launched the country on a steady course . . . that made it a much-admired model in Latin America and continued even after the dictator finally turned over the presidency (though not control of the armed forces) to an elected Christian Democrat in 1990."

"History of Latin America," *Encyclopaedia Britannica*

9. Since the 1980s, many countries in Latin America have moved politically toward

    (A) communism

    (B) representative democracy

    (C) nationalistic fundamentalism

    (D) totalitarianism

10. Pinochet's dictatorship persisted in Chile longer than many Latin American countries because

    (A) the people were satisfied with the economic situation

    (B) the communist regime punished dissension severely

    (C) the Sandinista party remained very popular

    (D) the government had financial backing from the Soviet Union

Part B: Key Topics

This key topics list is the same as the list in the Test What You Already Know section earlier in this chapter. Based on what you have now learned, ask yourself the following questions:

- Can I describe this key topic?
- Can I discuss this key topic in the context of other events?
- Could I correctly answer a multiple-choice question about this key topic?
- Could I correctly answer a free-response question about this key topic?

Check off the key topics if you can answer "yes" to at least three of these questions.

World War I

- ☐ League of Nations
- ☐ Mohandas Gandhi
- ☐ Total war
- ☐ World War I

Global Depression

- ☐ Great Depression
- ☐ World War II

Rise of Fascist and Totalitarian States

- [ ] Adolf Hitler
- [ ] Benito Mussolini
- [ ] Fascism
- [ ] Joseph Stalin

World War II

- [ ] Cold War
- [ ] Firebombing
- [ ] Nuclear bomb
- [ ] United Nations

The Cold War

- [ ] European Union
- [ ] Non-Aligned Movement
- [ ] Proxy wars
- [ ] Vietnam
- [ ] Warsaw Pact

Revolutions

- [ ] Fidel Castro
- [ ] Great Leap Forward
- [ ] Mao Zedong
- [ ] Vladimir Lenin

Independence and Nationalist Movements

- [ ] Algeria
- [ ] Ho Chi Minh
- [ ] Indian National Congress
- [ ] Indian/Pakistan Partition
- [ ] Muhammad Ali Jinnah

Political Reform and Economic Changes

- [ ] Deng Xiaoping
- [ ] NATO
- [ ] Tiananmen Square

Technology, Populations, and the Environment

- [ ] Cholera
- [ ] Green Revolution
- [ ] HIV/AIDS

Social and Cultural Changes

- [ ] Liberation theology in Latin America
- [ ] Pan-Africanism

1900 C.E. to Present

Tally Your Results for Part A and Part B

Part A: Check your answers and count the number of questions you got correct.

1.	B	6.	A
2.	C	7.	B
3.	C	8.	A
4.	B	9.	B
5.	C	10.	A

_____ out of 10 questions

Part B: Count the number of key topics you checked off.

_____ out of 36 key topics

Next Step: Compare your Test What You Already Know results to these Test What You Learned results to see how exam-ready you are for AP World History Period 6: 1900 to the Present.

Quiz Explanations

CHAPTER 3

Test What You Already Know

1. C

Stretching across modern-day Syria and through Iraq, the Tigris–Euphrates river system surrounds the areas once known as the Fertile Crescent. This river system allowed the Mesopotamian civilization to flourish. Therefore, **(C)** is correct. (A), (B), and (D) are all incorrect because they mismatch the rivers to their geographic areas, as shown in the map. The Nile River runs through Egypt, the Indus River runs through India and Pakistan, and the Huang He (Yellow) River is in China.

2. A

The Egyptian, Mesopotamian, and Indus Valley civilizations all had polytheistic religions, in which the supreme gods and goddesses controlled the forces of nature; a common characteristic for civilizations that relied on agriculture. The Chinese civilization, however, had a religion based on ancestor worship; there was no uniform system of religion. Because the question asked for a feature *common to all four* civilizations, **(A)** is the correct answer. All four of the civilizations thrived during the Bronze Age, generally considered to fall between 3000 B.C.E. and 1000 B.C.E. Further, archaeological evidence confirms that bronze was made and used in all four civilizations. Therefore, (B) is incorrect. Archaeologists have uncovered samples of writing in which pictures or symbols depicted specific concepts, including Egyptian hieroglyphics, Sumerian cuneiform, the Harappan Seals of the Indus Valley, and Chinese oracle bone inscriptions. Thus, (C) is incorrect. All four civilizations had varying degrees of social stratification. Generally, leaders and their advisers were at the top, followed by scholars, professionals, merchants, artisans, laborers, and the lower classes. (D) is incorrect.

3. D

The Nile River, noted for its dangerous rapids called "cataracts," was the backbone of the Ancient Egyptian civilization. Along with the Sahara Desert and the Mediterranean Sea, the Nile River provided an effective barrier against outside invaders due to its limited navigability. Therefore, **(D)** is the correct answer. The Huang He, although it deposited mineral-rich loess soil, often flooded violently and unpredictably, killing millions. The river is nicknamed "China's Sorrow" for this very reason. Thus, (A) is incorrect. The Indus Valley Civilization's main cities were located far away from central India, the source of the Ganges; further, the Indus Valley Civilization developed largely in isolation from the rest of the Indian subcontinent. Therefore, (B) is incorrect. The map clearly shows the Tigris and Euphrates Rivers emptying into the Persian Gulf, which allowed easy access to Arabia, Persia, and beyond. Indeed, archaeological evidence confirms that Sumerian traders used riverboats and "gulf boats" to travel as far as the Indus Valley. Thus, (C) is incorrect.

4. D

Mohenjo-Daro and Harappa were the most notable cities in the Indus Valley Civilization, centered in modern-day Pakistan and India. The ruins were discovered in the 1920s and are still being studied by archaeologists today. **(D)** is the correct answer. An example of an old oasis town along the Silk Road would be Samarkand, not Mohenjo-Daro and Harappa; (A) is incorrect. The dominant Ancient Greek city-states were Athens and Sparta, making (B) incorrect. An example of a port city along the Mediterranean basin would be Alexandria; (C) is incorrect.

5. A

The Harappan seals—metal and clay tiles featuring engraved images of animals and a script—remain undeciphered to this day. Linguists and archaeologists believe that translating these seals would help unlock the secrets of the Indus Valley Civilization. Therefore, **(A)** is correct. These cities are two of the earliest-known examples of urban planning and public sanitation. Therefore, (B) and (C) are incorrect. (D) is incorrect because the proximity of these cities to the Indus River not only provided the water needed to grow crops like wheat and cotton, but also provided a means to ship these goods elsewhere.

6. A

Both the Twelve Tables and Hammurabi's Code reflected the social structure of ancient societies, where a ruling elite occupied a privileged position above commoners. Thus, **(A)** is correct. While religious morality evolved alongside legal codes, they were not the primary motivation for social stratification. While the Roman Republic did, for a period, see its leadership bound by the rule of law, the first Babylonian empire was not a republic. Thus, (C) is incorrect. Both the Roman Republic and the first Babylonian empire were growing, internally stable bodies. They were not undergoing societal collapse; (D) is incorrect.

7. B

The Twelve Tables and Hammurabi's Code both embodied the idea that "the punishment should fit the crime." Indeed, the excerpts both display that more severe crimes were punishable by death. Further, both documents reference retaliation—the saying "an eye for an eye and a tooth for a tooth" originated in Hammurabi's Code. For these reasons, **(B)** is correct. Hammurabi expected his subjects to settle disputes through the Code itself, often using retaliation. Principles that are used in courtrooms today originated in the Twelve Tables. Therefore, (A) is incorrect. Both documents show that the wealthy paid fines for committing crimes that caused lower classes to be punished more severely. Thus, (C) is incorrect. Both legal codes made clear that a woman was to be subservient to her husband and to her home. (D) is incorrect.

8. B

Both of the excerpts reference the idea that "no one is above the law." Prior to the development of written legal codes, laws were arbitrary and the lower classes were often subjected to the abuses of the wealthy and powerful. By creating systems of uniform law that applied to everyone everywhere, the Twelve Tables and Hammurabi's Code both gave the lower classes rights that they had not had before; therefore, **(B)** is correct. (A) is incorrect because this statement only applies to the Twelve Tables; Hammurabi had vowed that anyone who changed, defiled, or destroyed his laws would be cursed. (C) is incorrect because only Republican Rome was ruled as a limited democracy, unlike Babylon, which was ruled by a king. (D) is incorrect because this statement only applies to Hammurabi's Code, which unified both Semitic and Sumerian ideas. The Twelve Tables were not intended to unify or change old customs.

9. A

In both Christianity and Buddhism, women could live the life of a nun. The Biblical excerpt illustrates the concept of becoming a nun. The Buddhist poem describes the transformation of a courtesan into a nun; for both, the aim is the same: seeking spiritual purity while being free from the traditional roles of wifehood and motherhood. For this reason, **(A)** is the correct answer. (B) is

incorrect because both religions considered women to be spiritual equals to men, despite socially delineated gender roles. (C) and (D) are both incorrect for a similar reason: the messages of both Christianity and Buddhism appealed to women. Both religions attracted female converts through their egalitarian ideals and their tales of holy men and holy women. Similarly, both Christian and Buddhist women were empowered to read spiritual texts (recall that Hindu women were not allowed to read the Vedas, and that Buddhism was created as an alternative to Hinduism).

10. D

As Christianity spread through the Mediterranean Basin, and as Buddhism spread through Asia, people started questioning the true nature of their respective founders. Consequently, different divisions of Christianity and Buddhism emerged, many of which are still practiced. For example, Nestorian Christians believed that Christ contained two distinct qualities, human and divine, rather than those two qualities being unified. Similarly, Theravada Buddhists consider the Buddha unique while Mahayana Buddhists believe he is merely one of many Buddhas. This similarity makes **(D)** the correct answer. (A) is incorrect because only Christianity is a religion of salvation; Christians believe that eternal life in Heaven is their ultimate goal, while Buddhists believe that nirvana, a state of perfect peace signified by breaking free from reincarnation, is their goal. (B) is incorrect because only Christianity are monotheistic while Buddhists feel that they can seek enlightenment without divine guidance. (C) is incorrect because it directly contradicts the correct answer; Buddhists do not see Buddha as both fully divine and fully human, and Christians only accepted this idea after the Council of Nicaea met in 325 C.E. and issued the Nicene Creed.

Test What You Learned

1. C

While currency as we know it today emerged in the Kingdom of Lydia (modern-day Turkey) around 600 B.C.E. with the creation of metal coins, paper currency was not developed until the seventh century C.E. under the Tang dynasty. Thus, **(C)** is correct. The rise of nomad confederations influenced the growth of trade along the Silk Road, as the Han dynasty sought to acquire horses that could put them on more equal footing with those ridden by the people on their periphery, and to separate potential nomadic allies in modern-day Mongolia and Tibet. Thus, (A) is incorrect. Knives and swords were known to exist as far back as 7000 B.C.E., but bronze smelting began around 2800 B.C.E., and iron metallurgy began in 1500 B.C.E. under the Hittites. Therefore, (B) is incorrect. Many of the earliest civilizations were built on trade; to keep accurate records, writing systems developed independently in many major civilizations. (D) is incorrect, as the earliest known example is cuneiform, the wedge-shaped writing of Mesopotamia.

2. D

The fall of the Western Roman Empire is only minimally due to foreign invasion, as the Romans had successfully fended off many such attacks in the past. Instead, the Roman Empire had been internally weakened ahead of the invasions. The breakdown of the tax and trade systems, political instability, the death of large numbers of the population due to disease, and the inability to recruit citizens to serve in the Legions leading to the hiring of Germanic mercenaries—all these factors weakened the Roman Empire enough for it to collapse when faced with a traditional challenge. Thus, **(D)** is correct. The Phoenicians were successively conquered by the Babylonians, Persians, and Macedonians. Finally, they and their colonies were absorbed by the Romans. Thus, (A) is incorrect. The exact cause of the downfall of the Minoans around 1450 C.E. is disputed, but is widely thought to be due to an earthquake, volcanic eruption, or other natural disaster. As these are natural causes and not internal problems, (B) is incorrect. The Gupta Empire suffered an invasion by the Huns, which fatally weakened it. This is the reverse of the Western Roman Empire. Thus, (C) is incorrect.

3. A

The ancient world provided modern society with many valuable contributions in virtually every field. The idea of a direct democracy, in which people directly influence laws through voting and active participation, originated in the sixth or fifth centuries B.C.E. in the Greek city-states. The very first democracy is a matter of speculation, but Athens, while its system came later in 508 or 507 B.C.E., is the most lasting and influential example. Since the question asked for an incorrect pairing, **(A)** is the correct answer. Rome was not a direct democracy but instead a republic. (B), (C), and (D) are all proper pairings. Paper as we know it was first manufactured in China between 179 B.C.E. and 105 C.E., and it quickly spread throughout the known world thereafter. Bronze, an alloy of copper and tin, was first smelted in Mesopotamia around 3000 B.C.E. Other civilizations perfected this powerful alloy to build tools and weapons in the following centuries. Because of the predictable flooding cycle of the Nile River, and a knowledge of astronomy, the Egyptians were able to create a 12-month, 30-day calendar with designated seasons based on the solar cycle.

4. D

Confucianism stressed the importance of harmony and order in relationships, focusing on five fundamental ones: ruler and subject, parent and child, husband and wife, siblings, and between friends. An alternate way to approach this question is to remember that Confucianism stresses the importance of filial piety as well as political stability. However, **(D)** refers to a religious relationship, and Confucianism is not considered a religion. (A), (B), and (C) are counted among the fundamental Confucian relationships.

5. D

In both Confucianism and Hinduism, scholars are highly regarded. Thus, **(D)** is correct. The highest caste in Hinduism is the Brahmin class, which consists of priests and scholars. Confucius taught that learning separated the inferior man from the superior man. Peasants were rarely educated and, in Hinduism, were part of the very lowest caste; (A) is incorrect. Artisans, while possibly educated, were part of the second-lowest caste, the Vaisyas, along with merchants and farmers. Therefore, (B) is incorrect. Government officials were part of the Kshatriyas, the second-highest caste, which included rulers, administrators, and warriors. Thus, (C) is incorrect.

6. D

Ashoka was an emperor of the Mauryan Dynasty (322–180 B.C.E.) in India who, after witnessing a bloody battle and feeling great sorrow and regret that the relatives of the dead would have to suffer, converted to Buddhism. Ashoka then issued a series of edicts that reference *dharma*. Thus, **(D)** is correct. Sikhism was founded in the fifteenth century C.E., well after the end of the Mauryan Dynasty; (A) is incorrect. Ashoka wanted to counteract the rising influence of the caste system, a key tenet of Hinduism; (B) is incorrect. Zoroastrians have long been a minority in India, where they today belong to either the Parsi or Irani communities. (C) is incorrect.

7. C

In Ashoka's time, the Brahmin, the priestly and highest caste of Hinduism, was experiencing greater power. Buddhism was designed to reject the caste system, and by centralizing his government, Ashoka displaced the Brahmin in favor of a more egalitarian belief system. Therefore, **(C)** is correct. Ashoka converted to Buddhism after suffering the effects of a bloody war. He reinforced the Aryan reverence of cattle by prohibiting animal slaughter, leading to the modern Indian belief in the sanctity of the cow. Therefore, (A) is incorrect. Over thirty engraved tablets and columns have been found throughout South Asia; furthermore, Ashoka funded the construction of shrines called *stupas*, where Buddhist relics are kept. Thus, (B) is incorrect. The spread of Buddhism along the Silk Roads started when Ashoka sponsored missions to present-day Nepal, Pakistan, and Afghanistan. (D) is incorrect

8. B

After the fall of Rome, nomadic invasions continued, making it very difficult for the area to recover. As a result, a decentralized form of government developed that provided protection for its inhabitants. Thus, **(B)** is correct. Both Rome and the Han permanently lost political control of their respective empires; thus, (A) and (D) are incorrect. Rome's population decreased as a result of the spread of disease, rather than increasing as (C) indicates.

9. A

The Han dynasty was rife with dynastic intrigue, with many emperors deposed. Actual power often resided in whichever group had helped secure the throne for young puppet emperors. Thus, **(A)** is correct. While regencies could in theory provide stable government, they often exposed the dynasty to more infighting as different groups sought to install child emperors and rule through them; thus, (B) is incorrect. It cannot be inferred that the dynastic line was an unbroken patrilineal line, and the youth of so many emperors makes such an arrangement unlikely, eliminating (C). Religious beliefs and popular sentiments played no part in the installation of such young emperors; thus, (D) is incorrect.

10. C

The Yellow Turban Rebellion (184–205 C.E.) was a peasant revolt in Han China. Therefore, **(C)** is correct. Along with numerous other factors, such as political corruption and infighting at the highest levels of government, this rebellion contributed to the downfall of the Han dynasty. As the rebellion was confined strictly to opposing Han rule in China, (A), (B), and (D) are incorrect.

CHAPTER 4

Test What You Already Know

1. B

Both the Roman Empire and the Mongol Empire established periods of economic and political stability; **(B)** is correct. These periods, known as the *Pax Romana* and *Pax Mongolica*, enabled trade to flourish within a large zone of common administration. The Romans, at their maximum extent, ruled all of Europe save Germany and owned minimal territory in Asia. The Mongols never extended their control past Central Europe. Thus, (A) is incorrect. Both empires were primarily land-based powers; (C) is incorrect. While the Roman Empire spread Latin as a common language, leading to the rise of various daughter languages, like French, after the fall of Rome, the Mongols did not forcibly spread their own language throughout their empire. Therefore, (D) is incorrect.

2. D

Both the Turks and Mongols were nomads who originated from the Central Asian steppes, making **(D)** correct. Although the Mongols conquered Korea and made it into a semi-independent vassal, the Turks have never invaded Korea. The Mongols were not skilled administrators, often using local people to help them rule, which eliminates (B). While the Ottoman Turkish alphabet was based on Arabic, the Mongolian alphabet was not; therefore, (C) is incorrect.

3. B

The Mongol Empire was vast and did not long survive the death of Kublai Khan. Though they were skilled military conquerors, civil war resulted from political rivals fighting over the right to become the next Great Khan. Thus, **(B)** is correct and (C) is incorrect. The Mongols were largely tolerant of native religious beliefs among their conquests; thus, (A) is incorrect. While the Red Turbans overthrew the Yuan dynasty in China, the rest of the former Mongol Empire had fractured by that point into several states. These other states were largely unaffected by that revolt. Therefore, (D) is incorrect.

4. C

Consider both the key details of the sources and your own knowledge of West African kingdoms. Both sources refer to Mansa Musa's practice of Islam. The second source also notes his desire to further spread Islam throughout his kingdom. The other key detail concerns Mansa Musa's wealth: Source 1 references his "prodigal spending" to the extent that gold "depressed its value in Egypt." These details together indicate **(C)**.

5. D

As trade between regions increases, ideas and religions typically spread as well. Likewise, the spread of a religion or philosophy across cultures often leads to increased economic relations as well. In this specific question, as a result of the spread of Islam into West Africa, the volume of trade along the trans-Saharan trade routes increased. Relationships were established with Muslim merchants and those relationships led to more trade, making **(D)** correct. The other answer choices reflect the opposite of what tends to occur when cultures increase contact. West Africa's economy grew rather than slowed, as suggested by (A), and a more centralized form of government administered the growing economy, as in (B). Centralized governments often kept order in their kingdoms, and thus decreased internal conflict, eliminating (C).

6. B

During the Crusades, Western Europe's elites personally experienced the diverse luxury goods and literature of the Eastern Roman Empire and the Muslim caliphate. This, plus increased shipping capacity for troop movements, boosted the already-growing trade volumes with the eastern Mediterranean, and led to an increase in interaction with all the civilizations to the south and east of the European peninsula. Therefore, **(B)** is correct. While navigational technology improved in Europe due to the Crusades, (A) incorrectly credits Europe with full control of all the Muslim lands of Asia Minor, Syria, and Palestine. (C) misstates the reason for the Crusades' weakening of feudalism; it was not that peasants saw worse conditions elsewhere, it was that the knightly class loosened its hold on its landed estates by prolonged absences, war deaths, and sales to raise travel funds. The idea of (D), that the Crusades were a serious economic blow to Europe, goes too far; the expenses and losses of waging these unprofitable foreign wars were serious but not enough to cancel out, much less reverse, the improvements in farming and trade productivity that had taken place since the fall of Rome.

7. D

The Eastern Roman Empire had been fighting the Islamic armies for centuries, and had hoped the Western crusaders would join with them in a Christian coalition. But in 1204, in a climax to increasingly hostile relations following the Great Schism, crusaders sacked and took over the imperial capital of Constantinople. **(D)** is correct. The Byzantines recaptured the city, but afterwards they were both weakened in their resistance to Islamic pressure and intensely resentful of the Roman Catholic West. (A) distorts the Byzantine policy of negotiating with Muslim states to try to stabilize borders between wars; it falsely implies that the emperor fought with the Turks against the crusaders. Byzantium had a longtime interest in retaking its lost provinces in the Levant, but (B) mistakenly credits it with the temporary successes of the Latin armies in reasserting Christian rule in the Holy Lands. Thus, (B) is incorrect. The Great Schism between the Orthodox and Catholic Christian rites took place in 1054, before the Crusades. Therefore, (C) is incorrect.

8. C

The frequency of cultural transfers between hostile groups in this period reminds us that warfare and conquests in history have a strong economic basis. Victors who seized or defended a throne usually favored continued trade to increase the taxable wealth of their realms. The Mongols established the most extensive land empire in history in the thirteenth century C.E.; at its height, it reached from China to Eastern Europe. Therefore, **(C)** is correct. The ruling Mongol dynasties facilitated peaceful trade across all of Asia so that China and the Muslim world were in closer contact than usual during this period. For example, the Chinese learned from Islamic math and astronomy; the Muslims received Chinese innovations like block printing and gunpowder. (A) and (B) are correct, but only for a later period in world history; the question is limited to the time of the Crusades. While the Teutonic and other wars of conversion in the pagan Baltic regions were part of the crusade movement, any implication that Jewish religious culture became important to entirely Christian regions ignores the marginal role of Judaism in medieval European culture. Thus, (D) is incorrect.

9. A

(A) is correct because Zheng He made as many as seven long-distance sea voyages during his illustrious career serving the Ming dynasty in China, as illustrated by the dated arrows on the map. (B) is not validated by the map because it does not depict the Silk Route, and (C) and (D) are speculative statements that cannot be supported using the information presented in the map.

10. D

Confucian officials in the court of the Ming emperor believed that the voyages of Zheng He were too expressive and not worth the cost of investment, as the money could be better spent elsewhere in the realm. This is comparable to the downfall of the Mali Empire, as a series of kings that spent lavishly spurred internal unrest and the collapse of their empire. Thus, **(D)** is correct. The Mongol conquest of Song China took many decades and was a hard-fought conflict, which does not reflect either party weakened by excessive spending. Thus, (A) is incorrect. The rise of the Umayyad dynasty was the result of a militarily efficient and politically cohesive state, as it faced regional rivals that required care to defeat. Thus, (B) is incorrect. The 1204 C.E. sack of Constantinople primarily resulted from a sectarian religious conflict between Latin Christians and Roman Catholics. Therefore, (C) is incorrect.

Test What You Learned

1. C

These two religions came in contact along the trade routes of Central Asia; **(C)** is correct. Buddhism had spread to the region earlier from India along the Silk Road. Islam spread to Central Asia beginning in the eighth century C.E. and often overtook Buddhism as the dominant belief system. Although Islam was present in the Spanish and Balkan peninsulas, Buddhism had almost no presence in

Europe in this period except for reports from travelers to Asia. Thus, (A) and (D) are incorrect. Some Buddhist Indian traders may have interacted with Muslim merchant communities in the Red Sea and Egyptian regions, which border on East Africa, but that kind of casual contact is a less correct choice for a question that refers to the religions as major institutions. Therefore, (B) is incorrect.

2. D

The passage suggests that despite their considerable theological differences, Islam and Buddhism shared a social and cultural appeal to the worldly middle class of traders and businessmen, who could be found all across the Eurasian continent in the first millennium C.E. Thus, as **(D)** says, the two faiths' encounter when Islam drove east in the eighth century led to a long-drawn competition of sorts, in which Islam's more aggressive aspects gave it a popular advantage in many regions that had been largely Buddhist. (A) is more descriptive of a political or economic competition between long-established nations. Although Islam and Buddhism did affect each other, the exchanges were artistic and cultural, and the two faiths did not converge. (B) and (C) are incorrect.

3. B

Baghdad was a city along the Silk Road, making **(B)** correct. The Mediterranean Sea, trans-Saharan routes, and Indian Ocean basin were common trade routes as well, but Baghdad was not located along any of them, making (A), (C), and (D) incorrect.

4. A

As the map of Baghdad includes water canals and land roads, trade in the Eastern Hemisphere occurred through land and water trade routes; thus, **(A)** is correct. Although disease pathogens, religious beliefs, and technologies did diffuse along trade routes, (B), (C) and (D) are incorrect because they are not supported by the map.

5. D

Baghdad trade was one destination along the Silk Road trade route. The Silk Road was not as significantly involved in the spread of Christianity as it was in the spread of Islam. Thus, **(D)** is correct. The bubonic plague and Chinese artwork such as porcelain did indeed spread along the Silk Road; therefore, (A) and (B) are incorrect. Travelers such as Marco Polo wrote as they migrated along the Silk Road. Thus, (C) is also incorrect.

6. B

Government support of industry did not take place until after the Industrial Revolution in the eighteenth and nineteenth centuries; thus, **(B)** is correct. Rather, commercial growth during the years 600 to 1450 C.E. was facilitated by the minting of coins (A), the establishment of trade organizations such as the Hanseatic League (C), and state-sponsored infrastructure projects, such as the construction of the Grand Canal in China (D).

7. C

The Red Turban Rebellion, an uprising of Chinese peasants upset over Mongol domination and high taxation, best reflects Voltaire's idea of a historical cycle where the elite are overthrown by an underclass that subsequently become the new elite. The Mongols had once been steppe nomads poor enough that they were forced to make clothes from the pelts of field mice. Now, even with the fragmentation of their empire, they ruled China under the banner of the Yuan dynasty. Zhu Yuanzhang, a peasant turned Red Turban, would overthrow them and become the first Ming emperor. Therefore, **(C)** is correct. The Kamakura shogunate was established by Japanese nobles who took power from rival elites; thus, (A) is incorrect. The Ghana Empire arose organically from villages along a trade network; thus, (B) is incorrect. The Byzantine Empire arose from a political reorganization of the faltering Roman Empire, and can be seen as existing in continuity with it. Indeed, the Byzantines would refer to themselves as Romans. Thus, (D) is incorrect.

8. A

Temujin, better known as Genghis Khan, feared that the Mongol Empire he had founded would dissolve into civil war over the question of his successor, as had repeatedly happened with steppe nomad confederations in the past. To that end, prior to his death, he clearly outlined who would be the next Great Khan and arranged for an equitable division of territory to his other sons, so none of them would feel slighted. Therefore, **(A)** is correct. The Mongols did not adopt a unifying religion in Temujin's era; (B) is incorrect. Tang China had dissolved into rebellion centuries before the rise of the Mongols. Thus, (C) is incorrect. The *Pax Mongolica* did not represent an effort to avoid a succession crisis after Temujin's death, but rather was a result of Temujin's lifetime of conquest. Thus, (D) is incorrect.

9. B

The Tang dynasty reformed the civil service examination to allow for the entry of gentry and commoners, and dispensed with the recommendation requirement that had allowed Han dynasty aristocrats to consolidate power among their families. Thus, **(B)** is correct. The Song dynasty would favor the tribute system over a strong military. The Tang dynasty was overthrown, in part, because military governors were strong enough to ignore the emperor. Thus, (A) is incorrect. While upper-class women in Tang China had more rights than in most other dynasties, this was not a top-down reform intended to correct a fault that had led to both injustice and the downfall of the previous dynasty. Thus, (C) is incorrect. Buddhism was downplayed in favor of Neo-Confucianism, which itself was a reaction to the upsurge of popularity of Buddhism, seen in China as a foreign philosophy. (D) is incorrect.

10. D

The Mali and the Mongols lacked a policy of forcibly converting their subjects; thus, **(D)** is correct. The Mongols had no unifying religion throughout their empire. The Mali rulers supported Islam but allowed their subjects to follow other faiths. Trade flourished in both empires. Thus, (A) is incorrect. Both empires also collected taxes from conquered regions; (B) and (C) are incorrect. Mali famously defeated the Sosso at the landmark Battle of Kirina, allowing the Malians to absorb them and territories of the former Ghana Empire.

CHAPTER 5

Test What You Already Know

1. A

The Chinese economy was the world's largest in this period, but the country lacked domestic silver or gold resources. This had led to the earliest invention of paper money, but misuse of that currency resulted in an inflationary spiral in the Ming Dynasty in the late 1400s—just as Japan and then Spanish America discovered and exploited their large silver reserves. China stabilized its money by switching from paper to silver. This led to a great demand for silver over the next few centuries. Therefore, **(A)** is correct. As the map shows, although most New World silver seems to be exported to Europe, a large fraction of it was then traded further east, to China, for the luxury goods that could not be paid for with any other exchange. (B) is contradicted by the map: the world's largest sources of silver were the mines in Spanish Peru and Mexico. Although some silver passed through Ottoman lands and seas in the course of world trade, as in (C), the Silk Road routes were increasingly bypassed by European ships trading silver for Chinese goods directly by sea. Ironically, given its inflationary history with paper money, the Ming dynasty actually experienced serious inflation due to an excessive importation of silver. As high inflation does not strengthen any economy, (D) is incorrect.

2. B

The silver trade was a primary component in the first truly global trade system, so called because of the growing unification of the Eastern and Western hemispheres' economies after European expansion. **(B) is correct.** This is best illustrated by the small but significant trade route across the Pacific Ocean between Mexico, Peru, the Philippines, and China—the first to connect the New World with the eastern and western halves of the Old World. Spain did not modernize internally despite its huge reserves of precious metals from America. Rather, it continued subsidizing its elite landholding classes and paying cash for talented foreigners to conduct its trade, imperial administration, and imperial wars. Thus, (A) is incorrect. (C) mixes up its history: the Opium Wars were in the 1800s, and sought to balance the silver trade between England and China, not end it. It is true that, as silver became available in large quantities, gold declined somewhat in relative value as in (D); however, that had little to do with the expansion of the slave trade in this period, which was based on demand for plantation commodities paid for with manufactured goods.

3. B

Unlike Portugal, whose royal government financed all of its expeditions in the Indian Ocean, the relatively impoverished British rulers used joint-stock companies, in which prosperous investors—not the crown—funded the expeditions. Thus, **(B) is correct.** As Roe's letter says, this allowed the English captains to separate the idea of controlling monopoly territories (e.g., by setting up expensive fortified trading stations) from the concept of seeking the best markets and trading agreements with local powers. Other factors in England's rise were its

generally stronger trading economy in the Atlantic and its successful competitions with France and the Netherlands, and Portugal's struggle with Spain and its increasing focus on its profitable empire in Brazil and Africa. (A) is out of period and region: the Opium Wars were in the 1800s and China was not primarily engaged in Indian Ocean trade. Although the Ottoman Empire had trading links to the Indian Ocean via its provinces on the Red Sea and Persian Gulf, it had never been the dominant naval or political power across the entire ocean basin as stated. Thus, (C) is incorrect. As noted, the Portuguese over time focused more on their Atlantic and African imperial holdings, but Portugal only abandoned its colonial ports at Goa in India and Macau in China in the late twentieth century. Thus, (D) is incorrect.

4. C

Ironically, given the close of Roe's letter, the British East India Company eventually did invest in "garrisons and land wars in India" in the eighteenth century. By the 1800s, this had led to a monopolistic business empire that ruled India as a private venture, supported indirectly by British military and legal institutions. General abuses of Indian sovereignty, culture, and privileges led to the "Mutiny" of the Company's native troops (Sepoys) in 1857, a bloody and bitter episode now called the "Rebellion" by Indian nationalists. Thus, **(C) is correct.** Although the Rebellion was unsuccessful in expelling the British, it did lead to the fall of the Company. The British government took over India as an imperial possession of Queen Victoria, and ruled there directly for another 90 years. The "Boston Tea Party," a 1773 riot against the Company's tea monopoly, contributed to the American Revolution but certainly didn't cause it. Thus, (A) is incorrect. (B) took place in conjunction with British expansion in India, and the two European empires in Asia engaged in border conflicts called "The Great Game," but Russia's interest in its southern neighbors was not dependent on the vulnerability of India. (D) is incorrect; Australia was initially set up as a penal colony after the American revolution eliminated North America as a place for transporting English criminals.

5. A

(A) is correct because though the Church was still quite powerful during the Renaissance, the growing power of merchant families and increasing interest in rediscovering the Greco-Roman past led to increasingly secular attitudes. New humanist philosophies depicted man as creative and rational, and the printing revolution supported a corresponding rise in literacy and interest in gaining knowledge. Therefore, (B) and (C) are incorrect. While attitudes were increasingly secular in outlook, stating that atheism become accepted by more and more Europeans goes too far. (D) is incorrect.

6. C

By supplying trade routes during the Crusades, Italy prospered immensely, making **(C)** correct. Additionally, contact with Eastern countries allowed for new ideas. (A) is not correct because Italy was a center of commerce. (B) is incorrect, as the Protestant Reformation took place after the Renaissance. Lastly, political power in Italy was characterized by many competitive city-states; thus, (D) is incorrect.

7. D

Europeans brought diseases such as measles and tuberculosis as they explored other regions, yet that is not depicted in the image. Therefore, **(D)** is correct. The horses and military apparel contained in the image demonstrate the transportation methods Spanish conquistadors used as they invaded; thus, (A) and (B) are incorrect. In the image, Cortés meets Xicotencatl, an indigenous leader who would ally with Cortés against Montezuma; therefore, (C) is incorrect.

8. B

In Aztec society, it was common for women to own property or involve themselves in religious traditions as priestesses, although these activities were uncommon in many other societies during that time period. Therefore, **(B)** is correct. Although the Aztec ruler did indeed claim that his rule was divinely inspired, because he himself had a divine origin, this assertion was relatively common, making (A) incorrect. Aztec society did incorporate slavery, and especially enslaved prisoners of war, and most Aztec commoners worked in agriculture, which makes (C) and (D) incorrect as well.

9. A

(A) is correct; both the Tokugawa shogunate and the French government under Louis XIV created laws to manage timber resources. Both (B) and (D) are true; however, they did not occur during the period from 1450 to 1750 C.E. The Ottoman Empire did not try to reduce overfishing. Therefore, (C) is incorrect.

10. C

Following an earlier period where Christianity was seen as a useful tool in combating the influence of Buddhism, the Tokugawa shogunate began to perceive Christianity as a threat to its authority and began persecuting missionaries. Thus, **(C)** is correct. Japan colonized Korea during the twentieth century, after the reign of the Tokugawa shogunate; (A) is incorrect. The Tokugawa shoguns did severely limit European trade with Japan; however, not all overseas trade was stopped. Carefully controlled trade with China, Korea, Taiwan and some Dutch merchants was allowed. Therefore, (B) is incorrect. The Tokugawa shogunate ensured very limited contact between Japan and the outside world. Thus, (D) is incorrect.

Test What You Learned

1. D

The Safavid and Mughal empires fell more than 100 years before the late 1800s when economic dependence on oil emerged, so **(D)** is correct. The Byzantine Empire held Constantinople, a city which was heavily fortified and considered impregnable. The utilization of firearms such as cannons, however, shifted the advantage to the side of the Ottomans, and Constantinople fell to the Turks. Similarly, the Safavid and Mughal empires conquered territories using similar techniques. Thus, (A) is incorrect. (B) and (C) are incorrect because all three empires were known for politically supporting Islam in addition to fostering artistic innovations and achievements.

2. B

All three empires (Ottoman, Safavid, Mughal) were controlled by Muslim rulers. However, the Ottomans practiced the Sunni branch of Islam while the Safavids believed in the Shi'ite branch of Islam. Therefore, **(B)** is correct. The Ottoman and Safavid empires contained religious minorities, namely Christians and Jews. Thus, (A) is incorrect. As all three empires were both dominated by the military classes and experienced warfare during times of succession, (C) and (D) are incorrect.

3. D

(D) is correct; neither China nor Europe focused resources on reconnaissance in the Pacific Ocean during this period. The Indian Ocean region (India, the Middle East, and the coast of Africa) was explored by Chinese maritime reconnaissance voyages, especially under Ming Admiral Zheng He. Thus, (A) is incorrect. The Portuguese set up trading post empires in West Africa; (B) is incorrect. The Spanish colonized large territories in South America; (C) is incorrect.

4. D

Ming rulers were not afraid of Europeans. Rather, they believed China to be superior to the West, with nothing to gain from the rest of the world. Therefore, **(D)** is correct. Ming leaders feared the impacts technological innovation would have on social order; (A) is incorrect. Confucian officials did argue against commercial activity; (B) is incorrect. The surviving Yuan Mongols did raid western China, demanding attention and resources. Thus, (C) is incorrect.

5. B

In order to demonstrate the subjugation of the Han Chinese people, the invading Manchus of the Qing dynasty decreed that all Chinese men should shave their heads and adopt the queue hairstyle of the Manchu and other northern cultures. This most visible indignity aroused great resistance among the Chinese across all classes and regions. Thus, **(B)** is correct. However, the new style was enforced ruthlessly, becoming a common characteristic of Chinese men until the twentieth century. The other answers are incorrect: the Manchus did not attempt to restrict foreign trade (A), compel intermarriage between the cultures (C), or remove the Confucian bureaucracy it had inherited from the Ming dynasty (D). On the contrary, the Confucian bureaucracy of Ming China was preserved and used to administer the empire as efficiently as ever.

6. C

The Manchus' imposition of a distinctive hairstyle on the Chinese was in order to change their traditional appearance and make them look more like the conquering or elite culture. The closest event to this is the elimination of the turban (and robed clothing style) in favor of a fez hat (and more Western-cut clothes) by the Turkish elites of the Ottoman Empire, who wished to Westernize their empire's various Islamic subcultures. Thus, **(C)** is correct. As with the queue, the fez became identified with Turkish appearance so much that its later abandonment was as difficult and revolutionary as its initial adoption. What is different is that this decree was not due to a conquest but to an internal conflict on how to respond to outside pressure. (A), (B), and (D) are all instances of elites using dress, appearance, and classification to separate

and control, rather than integrate and unify, subordinate classes or hierarchies.

7. C

The early Spanish settlers in the Caribbean needed a large labor force to exploit the area's resources. Europeans saw the inhabitants of useful land as part of the land's value. No thought was given to transplanting Spanish peasants to a New World which had a thriving native population. Instead, under the *encomienda* system that had been used during the reconquest of Muslim territories in Spain, the King gave Spanish colonists the right to compel the labor of local native peoples in their newly developed mines and plantations. Therefore, **(C)** is correct. Although the result of this system, combined with introducing foreign diseases, was to decimate the native populations within a few decades, that was certainly not the purpose of *encomienda* but instead a result. Thus, (A) is incorrect. The slave trade from Africa resulted from the attrition of native labor; the Spanish had no ethical concerns about limiting its increase. Thus, (B) is incorrect. Finally, it should be clear that *encomienda*'s purpose was to exploit the Native Americans, not give them economic opportunities. Therefore, (D) is incorrect.

8. A

Reading the passage closely and eliminating the other answer choices will lead you to the correct answer, **(A)**. (B) incorrectly assumes that the institution of African slavery was the result of a single royal decree in response to de las Casas's expose of the cruelty of *encomienda*. (C) is incorrect, as the Church did not take on such a role. (D) is incorrect because while de las Casas's report resulted in the New Laws of 1542, whereby the King decreed better treatment of natives and restricted the colonists' *encomienda* privileges, the answer incorrectly credits these reforms to the colonists themselves, who actually resisted the New Laws vigorously. (A) identifies the other and longer-lasting historical impact (beside the New Laws) of this book: it is one of the earliest works of the modern era to agitate for universal human rights and the dignity of slaves, laborers, and other oppressed classes of all cultures and races.

9. D

The Italian Renaissance (from the Latin word for "rebirth") was a period of social, political, and cultural learning and awareness that lasted from approximately from 1300 to 1600 C.E. During this time, wealthy families like the

Medicis ruled city-states and funded artists like Leonardo da Vinci. The geography of Italy enabled its city-states to take advantage of trading routes in the Mediterranean; **(D)** is correct. Ideas and goods from Italy spread into Northern Europe, sparking the Northern Renaissance there; however, artists and writers from that region include Rembrandt, Jan van Eyck, and Erasmus; therefore, (A) is incorrect. The Protestant Reformation is one of the outcomes of the Northern Renaissance, not the Italian Renaissance, as it began in Germany with Martin Luther's *95 Theses* in 1517. Therefore, (B) is incorrect. The Enlightenment was a continuation of ideas that originated during the Italian and Northern Renaissances; however, it occurred in the eighteenth and nineteenth centuries—much later than the lives of da Vinci and the Medici family. Therefore, (C) is incorrect.

10. A

Art and literature reflected the developments of the Italian Renaissance, which was characterized by an appreciation for realism and nature, an interest in the human body and its beauty, and an emphasis on reason and logical thought. Therefore, **(A)** is correct. During the Italian Renaissance, artists and writers did not focus strictly on religious imagery and influences. Thus, (B) is incorrect. While much of the artwork was religious in nature, artists also worked to revive ancient classics from the Greek and Roman civilizations. Though it is counterintuitive, women did not gain any new rights or freedoms during the Italian Renaissance; thus, (C) is incorrect. The Italian Renaissance drew inspiration from Ancient Greece and Rome, as well as the Islamic world. (D) is incorrect.

CHAPTER 6

Test What You Already Know

1. B

Slave trading with Europeans began in coastal regions of Africa, causing previously established African trade routes to shift; **(B)** is correct. North Africa remained predominantly Islamic despite European imperialism, while sub-Saharan Africa largely Christianized in the twentieth century, well after the end of the transatlantic slave trade. Thus, (A) is incorrect. Also, the map suggests that relatively little slave trading occurred in regions of Northern Africa such as Egypt and Algeria. It also suggests that relatively few slaves were sent to India and other Asian regions, and that relatively little slave trading occurred near Cape Colony in South Africa. Therefore, (C) and (D) are incorrect.

2. A

Although Islam did indeed spread throughout Africa during this time period, it had the least impact on the slave trade, making **(A)** correct. Influenced by Islamic and Asian technological developments, the Europeans improved ship design, utilized better navigation techniques, and produced goods such as gunpowder, which allowed them to more easily engage in global trade. Thus, (B) and (C) are incorrect. Once the Europeans established colonies in the Americas, they used slaves to provide labor in these regions. (D) is also incorrect.

3. B

Sugar was an especially labor intensive cash crop, meaning plantation owners required cheap labor. Their primary source of such labor was African slaves, who were transported to the Americas through the transatlantic slave trade. Therefore, **(B)** is correct. Industrialization began with the nineteenth century Industrial Revolution, postdating this map. Thus, (A) is incorrect. Although absolute monarchy was the primary political system in Europe during this period, it did not directly affect the economics of the slave trade. Therefore, (C) is incorrect. European countries of this time period adhered to mercantilist principles rather than laissez-faire capitalism; this meant that governments intervened in economic exchange by placing tariffs on goods from other countries and promoting industries within their countries, instead of allowing free market exchanges to occur. Thus, (D) is also incorrect.

4. C

Thomas Paine, the author of the popular pamphlet *Common Sense*, and other leaders of the American Revolution were inspired by Enlightenment philosophers—including Montesquieu, Locke, and Rousseau—to establish independence from England in the 1770s. These leaders were not primarily motivated by economic considerations. Therefore, **(C)** is correct. Charles Inglis, the Loyalist author of this passage, describes how the colonies' economic dependence on Great Britain should have otherwise deterred these leaders from embarking on such a risky revolution. (A) is incorrect; the Industrial Revolution did indeed begin in England, but it began in the 1780s, after the American Revolution had ended. Although the passage mentions metal, the American revolutionaries were not primarily motivated by a desire to improve the colonies' industries. Rather, more abstract ideas about natural rights and the social contract inspired them. Therefore, **(B)** is incorrect. (D) is also incorrect; it describes the Puritans' religious motivations to create their settlements in Massachusetts in the seventeenth century.

5. C

Although serfdom was no longer present in late eighteenth century France, many of the obligations and taxes of the feudal period continued to burden peasants up to the revolution. Thus, **(C)** is correct. Unlike the American Revolution, France's revolution was primarily an internal struggle resulting from dramatic social divisions and economic inequality. Thus, (A) is incorrect. While the wealthiest members of society were at the forefront of the American Revolution, the wealthy typically resisted the French Revolution, which was led primarily by the Third Estate. While a catch-all category for people who were not nobles or clergy, politically the Third Estate was primarily led by the *bourgeoisie*. Thus, (B) is incorrect. Enlightenment philosophers and ideals such as natural rights, the separation of powers, and the social contract inspired both revolutions. Therefore, (D) is incorrect.

6. A

The thirteen British colonies primarily provided England with their natural resources instead of growing their own industries. That model describes mercantilist principles; **(A)** is correct. Feudalism was a medieval social system which generally required peasants to serve vassals, who in turn served nobles. This does not describe the passage, so (B) is incorrect. Similarly, (C) is incorrect because monarchism is a political system, in which a monarch such as King George III of Great Britain rules over his people. Economic liberalism is a system which advocates for free trade and minimal government regulation of the economy, which contrasts with the limitations of mercantilist trade. Therefore, (D) is incorrect.

7. B

The Indian National Congress was a group of educated Indians formed with the permission of the British in the late nineteenth century. This group eventually helped to lead the nationalist movement in India under the leadership of Mohandas Gandhi. The Pan-African Congress first met in 1919 after World War I. It stressed African unity and

helped to create nationalist movements, which came to eventually defeat the European colonial powers. Therefore, **(B)** is correct, while (A), (C), and (D) are incorrect.

8. B

Toussaint L'Ouverture helped lead the Haitian revolution. Simón Bolívar led the establishment of Venezuela, Bolivia, Colombia, Ecuador, Peru, and Panama as sovereign states, free of Spanish rule. Miguel Hidalgo y Costilla was a leader of the Mexican War of Independence. Therefore, **(B)** is correct. The Reconquista refers to a series of wars and battles between Christian Kingdoms and Muslim Moors for control of the Iberian Peninsula during the Middle Ages. Thus, (A) is incorrect. All three leaders advocated for the abolishment of slavery and predated the mid-nineteenth-century development of communist ideology. (C) and (D) are incorrect.

9. D

Toussaint L'Ouverture led a successful slave revolt in Saint-Domingue, resulting in the independence of Haiti and abolition of slavery; **(D)** is correct and (C) incorrect. Prior to the revolt, France controlled Saint-Domingue, not the United States. Therefore, (A) is incorrect. Inspired by both Enlightenment ideals and the French Revolution, Haiti became the first democracy established in the Caribbean; (B) is incorrect.

10. A

The Sepoy Rebellion began after a rumor spread that gunpowder cartridges were made from cow and pig fat, which insulted Hindu and Muslim religious practices. In response, both Muslim and Hindu Indians rebelled cooperatively against British rule. Therefore, **(A)** is correct and (C) is incorrect. The Indian National Congress was instrumental in India's independence from Great Britain, but was formed after the Sepoy Rebellion; (B) is incorrect. After this war, the British East India Company no longer ruled India. Instead, the British crown ruled the subcontinent directly. Thus, (D) is incorrect.

Test What You Learned

1. C

John Locke argued that human beings have certain rights, such as the right to life, liberty, and property. Thus, **(C)** is correct. Since governments exist in order to protect these rights, if they fail to do so, they can be overthrown and replaced. As John Locke argued for the separation of church and state, (A) is incorrect. He did not believe humans are born with innate knowledge of truths. Instead, Locke felt that humans learned by experience; (B) is incorrect. (D) refers to a government system of communism, which John Locke did not argue for.

2. C

During the Revolutionary War, American generals often employed the use of guerrilla warfare tactics, an unconventional military strategy. Therefore, **(C)** is correct. The Franco-American alliance did provide both moral and military support to the colonists; (A) is incorrect. The British army wasn't large enough to occupy enough North American territory, giving Americans a "home field" advantage. Thus, (B) is also incorrect. American patriotism united colonists in the cause for freedom, making (D) incorrect.

3. A

The Seven Years' War put Britain into massive debt. In order to pay off the debt, the English government imposed new taxes on its colonies. Additionally, Britain ended its policy of salutary neglect in favor of strict enforcement of parliamentary laws. Therefore, **(A)** is correct while (C) is incorrect. During the war, France lost North American territory, including Quebec, to the English; (B) is incorrect. Before the war, Native American tribes had good relations with French traders in the area. After the war, however, tensions between Native Americans and the English escalated, prompting conflicts such as Pontiac's War. Thus, (D) is incorrect.

4. A

This Renaissance-style building, called the Rokumeikan or "Deer Cry Hall," was built during the Meiji period and became a symbol of Japanese westernization, making **(A)** correct. The social and political changes during the Meiji period arose due to pressure on Japan to keep pace with Western influence and industrialization. European trading companies such as the British East India Company did not control any Japanese cities; therefore, (B) is incorrect. (C) is incorrect as the Tokugawa shogunate used traditional Japanese architecture in constructing their palaces. The Showa era corresponds to the rule of Emperor Hirohito, who ruled from 1926 to 1989, which is long after the building pictured was built; therefore, (D) is incorrect.

5. B

Upon taking power, Emperor Meiji took an oath which declared, "We shall endeavour to raise the prestige and honor of our country by seeking knowledge throughout the world." After opening to Western influence, Japan sent its leaders abroad to learn about modern advances in military and manufacturing technology, making **(B)** correct. (A), (C), and (D) were all events and developments that did indeed occur during the Meiji restoration, which is the same era as the building's construction.

6. B

The nineteenth century saw contact and conflict between Western powers and East Asian empires which often turned violent, with the result of land ceded to Western powers, such as Britain. Emperor Meiji agreed to open trade not due to Commodore Perry's diplomatic tactics, but rather, the desire to avoid being forced into a trade relationship with the United States or worse, becoming a colony. Therefore, **(B)** is correct, and (A) is incorrect. Prior to Commodore Perry's arrival, Japan did not come into contact with or desire Western goods or technology, making (C) incorrect. (D) is incorrect as the shogun was overthrown in 1868 and replaced by the Emperor Meiji.

7. D

The Opium Wars most directly resulted in the weakening of Chinese sovereignty as it related to trade, as tariffs were removed and foreigners were granted special rights and privileges. Thus, **(D)** is correct. While the outbreak of the Taiping Rebellion resulted, in part, from the First Opium War, the rebellion was still ongoing when the Second Opium War broke out. Therefore, (A) is incorrect. The downfall of the shogunate and the restoration of the emperor describes the Meiji Restoration, which happened in Japan. Thus, (B) is incorrect. The Ottoman Empire adopted the French legal code and saw a soft takeover by the Young Turks; (C) is incorrect.

8. C

The Qing emperor declared that having a British diplomat come to his court to control trade with China would be unacceptable, or "contrary to all usage of my dynasty," matching **(C)**. He neither welcomed further foreign investment in his empire (A), nor stated that the British had any previous trading privileges that he would continue to uphold (B). The letter expressed polite gratitude to George III for sending an envoy so far, but did not reflect a submissive attitude. In fact, the closing statement encouraged George to embrace "perpetual submission to our Throne," reflective of the emperor's belief in China's superiority, so (D) is incorrect.

9. B

The Qing dynasty wanted very little commercial or cultural exchange with the outside world in the eighteenth century, continuing the isolationist policy of the previous Ming dynasty and matching **(B)**. Laissez-faire refers to totally unregulated trade, which does not fit with the emperor's resistance to opening trade with the British Empire, seen in the letter, so (A) is incorrect. China would not become a communist country until the post-imperial period, in 1949, eliminating (C). China was still a feudal empire at the time of the letter, so (D) is incorrect.

10. A

The French Revolution saw the internal revolt against a monarchy, the establishment of a republic, and eventually a failure of the initial revolution and rollback of its ideas. The Revolution of 1911, also called the Xinhai Revolution, likewise saw its gains rolled back as violence soon broke out and China descended into warlordism and civil war. Therefore, **(A)** is correct. The Paris Commune was a revolutionary socialist government. While one of Sun Yat-sen's Three Principles of the People was socialism, it was not as strident, and his revolution's Republic of China was not crushed by a large native army. Thus, (B) is incorrect. Sun Yat-sen took over his home country rather than fighting for independence from it. Thus, (C) is incorrect. The Young Turks installed a puppet sultan to rule through, while Sun Yat-sen and his fellow revolutionaries overthrew their own monarchy and established a republic.

CHAPTER 7

Test What You Already Know

1. B

Russia's rapid industrialization in the last decade of the nineteenth century resulted in poor living conditions for the working class. This led to the organization of new socialist parties, such as the Marxist Social Democratic Party and the Social Revolutionaries. In January of 1905, socialist protesters, led by the priest Georgy Gapon, marched to the Winter Palace in St. Petersburg; **(B)** is correct. (A) and (D) are incorrect because the Tanzimât reform movement was a reformation period of the Ottoman Empire, and the Self-Strengthening Movement was a series of reforms during the Qing dynasty in China, both occurring in the nineteenth century. Although witnesses to the demonstration in the passage described the protestors as being "not our people," the protestors were socialist and not anti-nationalist, making (C) incorrect.

2. D

The Russian Revolution of 1905 directly ignited strikes and uprisings throughout the nation, but it also more generally spurred Russian revolutionary efforts to continue. Thus, **(D)** is correct. After the Revolution of 1905, the tsar did form the Duma in 1906; however, this legislative assembly disbanded during the later Revolution of 1917, making (A) incorrect. (B) is incorrect because tsarist rule continued in Russia until the Revolution of 1917, culminating in the execution of the tsar and his family in 1918. (C) is incorrect because socialism continued to grow as the primary revolutionary movement in Russia after 1905.

3. D

Gender equality became a key principle of communist social organization after the Chinese Cultural Revolution; **(D)** is correct. Women were often depicted in masculine clothing, with short hair and severe features, performing traditional male work. (A) is incorrect because the image was directed at Chinese youth, not Taiwanese dissidents. While Mao did transplant urban youth to rural areas in the "Down to the Countryside" movement, it is not depicted in this image; (B) is incorrect. Mao did not actively wish to imitate Russia's approach to communism, making (C) incorrect.

4. A

(A) is correct because the Cultural Revolution sought to destroy anything that could undermine communist ideals, which in Mao's view included art and literature from previous periods in Chinese history. (B) describes the aims of the Great Leap Forward, which achieved limited success; therefore, it is incorrect. The Cultural Revolution sought to eliminate political dissent and restore power to Mao and his allies, making (C) incorrect. The Cultural Revolution aimed to eliminate what were known as the "Four Olds"—old customs, old culture, old habits, and old ideas—not restore them; therefore, (D) is incorrect.

5. D

The United Nations was formed in 1945 as a result of World War II, making **(D)** correct. Fifty-one countries started the international organization, which was committed to maintaining international peace and security, developing friendly relations among nations, and promoting social progress. The Korean War began in 1950, after the United Nations had been well established, making (A) incorrect. The Cold War refers to the tension between the Eastern Bloc (the Soviet Union and satellite nations) and the Western Bloc (the United States and its Western European allies), and lasted approximately from the end of World War II until the collapse of the Soviet Union in 1991; (B) is incorrect. The international organization founded after World War I to promote peace was called the League of Nations, making (C) incorrect.

6. A

The League of Nations, the organization preceding the United Nations, was doomed to fail when the United States and Soviet Union, two of the most powerful countries at the time, refused to join; **(A)** is correct. (B) is incorrect because, while the Great Depression did negatively affect the global economy, the League of Nations was not involved in international commerce enough to be affected. The League of Nations had no force, making it powerless in military conflicts; (C) is incorrect. The global spread of communism did not become a significant issue until after World War II, when the League of Nations was replaced by the United Nations; therefore (D) is also incorrect.

7. C

While the charter does generally reference economic relations between countries, international trade is not an explicit purpose of the UN itself; therefore, **(C)** is correct. The UN charter outlines its mission of promoting personal freedoms in the form of human rights, (A), preventing military aggression through diplomacy, (B), and increasing "friendly relations among nations based on respect for the principle of equal rights and the self determination of peoples" (D).

8. D

In 1960, most Latin American countries had some form of dictatorship, and democracy, where it existed, was not complete or fully expressed. By 2000, almost all countries in the Western Hemisphere, with the notable exceptions of Cuba and Haiti, had a functioning democracy, making **(D)** correct. Cuba was the only Latin American country at this time to adopt a communist government, so (A) is incorrect. The majority of Latin American military dictatorships were overthrown in this period, making (B) incorrect. Most European colonial control in Latin America ended in the early 1800s; (C) is incorrect.

9. C

The socialist Sandinista National Liberation Front, with members known as Sandinistas, ruled Nicaragua after deposing Somoza in 1979, matching **(C)**. At this time Fidel Castro ran the communist nation of Cuba, and Honduras and Guatemala were subject to numerous government upheavals, eliminating (A), (B), and (D).

10. A

After establishing a communist regime in Cuba, Fidel Castro developed a diplomatic relationship with the Soviet Union, receiving financial and military support; **(A)** is correct. Neither Brazil nor Spain provided significant support to Cuba during this period, eliminating (B) and (D). During the height of the Cold War in the second half of the twentieth century, the United States opposed Cuban and Soviet efforts to aid socialist and communist uprisings in Latin America; (C) is incorrect.

Test What You Learned

1. B

During World War I, ships like the *H.M.S. Orvieto* accompanied Allied civilian ships in order to protect them against German U-boat attacks. The Germans attempted to interfere with supply shipments to Allied powers. Due to the defensive strength provided by armed convoys, Allied powers did not suffer the kind of food and supply shortages that Central powers did under the British naval blockade; therefore, **(B)** is correct. (A) is incorrect, as German U-boats did not succeed in sabotaging civilian supply shipments enough to impact Allied powers. Though the British Empire was large and spanned multiple continents, the map does not depict them, making

(C) incorrect. Ironclad ships were developed and first used by the British navy in 1861, long before the outbreak of World War I; (D) is incorrect.

2. C

The increased demand for raw materials during World War I led to an economic boon for countries like Chile, whose nitrate exports were used as an ingredient in gunpowder; **(C)** is correct. (A) is incorrect because, in comparison to other American wars, not many American men evaded the draft. Latin American countries were not directly involved in the fighting, making (B) incorrect. (D) is incorrect because Latin America exported raw materials, not luxury goods.

3. C

Many colonial territories relied on exporting one or two main products, leaving them vulnerable to fluctuations in the global market. Global demand for rubber, for example, dramatically decreased during the Depression, due in part to a dip in car tire manufacturing. This was disastrous for colonial economies, making **(C)** correct. Both (A) and (D) are incorrect as the Great Depression did not directly lead to independence or communist revolution. This occurred more after World War II, when imperial governments were weakened. (B) is incorrect because all global trade and manufacturing contracted, lessening the need for finished goods and raw materials alike.

4. B

In response to the global economic crisis spurred by the Great Depression, many countries adopted a policy of economic protectionism, which included raising tariffs in order to restrict imports; therefore, **(B)** is correct. The Global Depression resulted in political unrest and extremism for many countries, a rise in global unemployment, and the collapse of world financial centers; (A), (C), and (D) are incorrect.

5. C

The Russian Bolsheviks gained most of their support from working-class individuals living in the cities, not rural areas. On the other hand, China had an enormous peasant population that was sympathetic to communist policies like land redistribution; **(C)** is correct. (A), (B), and (D) are incorrect because these were all commonalities between the two communist revolutions. Both Russia and China struggled with how to communize societies that were mainly agricultural and pre-industrial, and accordingly, instituted Five-Year Plans; Russia and China were also similar in their totalitarian methods, as both imprisoned and even killed those who opposed their new regime.

6. A

The Sino-Soviet split was a rift that grew from approximately 1956 to 1960 and continued into the 1980s between the Soviet Union and China, the two biggest communist powers in the world at that time. Its origins lay in Nikita Khrushchev's denunciation of Stalin and grew to include larger differences in interpretation of communist ideology, dealings with the capitalist West, and communism around the world; **(A)** is correct. (B) is incorrect as the Soviet Union and China did not have, nor compete for, overseas colonies. Differences in ideology and overall national interests ran far deeper than the fractious relationship between Khrushchev and Mao, making (C) incorrect. (D) is incorrect because the détente between the United States and the Soviet Union was an outcome of the Sino-Soviet split, not a cause.

7. B

In the mid-1980s, Soviet leader Mikhail Gorbachev initiated policies that would ultimately lead to the dismantling of the U.S.S.R. *Glasnost*, or "openness," referred to a policy of cultural and intellectual freedom, leading to increased freedom for the press. *Perestroika*, or "restructuring," introduced some aspects of capitalism into the existing economic system; **(B)** is correct. (A), (C), and (D) are all incorrect as Mao, Stalin, and Castro all did not permit government transparency or freedom for their citizens.

8. A

(A) is correct, as the reunification of Germany was a result of the collapse, due to the loss of Soviet control of East Germany. (B) is incorrect because the costly invasion of Afghanistan proved disastrous for the already-stretched Soviet economy. The Solidarity movement in Poland was an anti-communist social movement which successfully overthrew the communist government in 1989. The Soviet Union therefore lost one of its most important satellite states, and many others in similar revolutions in 1989; (C) is incorrect. (D) is incorrect, as implementing the policies of *glasnost* and *perestroika* weakened the tight control the Soviet Union had held over its citizens.

9. B

Several Latin American countries struggled politically and economically through destabilizing regime changes in the twentieth century, but most moved politically toward representative democracy beginning in the 1980s; **(B)** is correct. Communism remains limited in the region, fundamentalist regimes have not come to power, and most totalitarian dictatorships have been deposed; therefore, (A), (C), and (D) are incorrect.

10. A

By liberalizing markets and encouraging foreign loans and investment, Chile was able to create a much stronger economy than many other Latin American dictatorships, making **(A)** correct. The regime under Augusto Pinochet was anti-communist, so (B) is incorrect. The Sandinista party was active in Nicaragua, not Chile, eliminating (C). Pinochet's staunch persecution of communists meant that Chile did not ally with the Soviet Union, making (D) incorrect.

References

CHAPTER 2

Document-Based Question

Document 4

Mintzuri, Hagop. *Istanbul Anilari 1897–1940*, translated by Silva Kuyumcuyan. Istanbul: Tarih Vakfi, 2002.

CHAPTER 3

Test What You Learned (Post-Quiz)

Questions 1–3

Stokes Brown, Cynthia. "What is Civilization, Anyway?" *World History Connected*, 2009, http://worldhistoryconnected.press.illinois.edu/6.3/brown.html.

Questions 8–10

Zürcher, Erik and Denis C. Twitchett. "China." *Encyclopaedia Britannica, Inc.*, 2017, https://www.britannica.com/place/China/Dong-Eastern-Han.

CHAPTER 4

Test What You Already Know (Pre-Quiz)

Questions 6–8

Madden, Thomas F. *The New Concise History of the Crusades*. Rowman & Littlefield, 2005.

Test What You Learned (Post-Quiz)

Questions 1–2

Elverskog, Johan. *Buddhism and Islam on the Silk Road*. Philadelphia: University of Pennsylvania Press, 2010.

CHAPTER 5

Test What You Already Know (Pre-Quiz)

Questions 9–10

Lu, D. J. *Japan: A Documentary History*. London: Routledge, 1997.

Test What You Learned (Post-Quiz)

Questions 1–2

Marcus, Jacob. *The Jew in the Medieval World: A Sourcebook, 315-1791.* Cincinnati: Sinai Press, 1938.

Questions 5–6

Struve, L. A. *The Southern Ming, 1644–1662.* Yale University Press, 1984.

CHAPTER 7

Test What You Already Know (Pre-Quiz)

Questions 5–7

United Nations. Charter of the United Nations. 24 October 1945, 1 UNTS XVI, http://www.un.org/en/sections/un-charter/chapter-i/index.html.

Questions 8–10

Lockhart, James, Roger A. Kittleson, and David Bushnell. "History of Latin America." *Encyclopaedia Britannica, Inc.,* 2017, https://www.britannica.com/place/Latin-America.

Test What You Learned (Post-Quiz)

Questions 5–6

Zedong, Mao. "Outline for a Speech on the International Situation," December, 1959, *History and Public Policy Program Digital Archive,* http://digitalarchive.wilsoncenter.org/document/118893.

Questions 9–10

Lockhart, James, Roger A. Kittleson, and David Bushnell. "History of Latin America." *Encyclopaedia Britannica, Inc.,* 2017, https://www.britannica.com/place/Latin-America.